Debt Recovery in the Courts

Available titles in this series include:

Termination of Employment

John Bowers QC and Carol Davis

Residential Tenancies

Richard Colbey and Niamh O'Brien

Child Care and Protection

Barbara Mitchels with Helen James

Agricultural Tenancies

Angela Sydenham

Change of Name

Nasreen Pearce

Procedure in Civil Courts and Tribunals

John Bowers QC and Eleena Misra

Partnership and LLP Law

Elspeth Berry

 Wildy Practice Guides

Debt Recovery in the Courts

John Kruse

Wildy, Simmonds and Hill Publishing

© 2010 Wildy, Simmonds & Hill Publishing

The right of John Kruse to be identified as the author of this Work has been asserted by him in accordance with sections 77 and 78 of the Copyright, Designs and Patents Act 1988

First published in Great Britain 2010 by Wildy, Simmonds & Hill Publishing

Website: www.wildy.com

All rights reserved. No part of this publication may be reproduced, stored in a retrieval system, or transmitted, in any form or by any means, electronic, mechanical, photocopying, recording, scanning or otherwise, except under the terms of the Copyright Designs and Patents Act 1988 or under the terms of a licence issued by the Copyright Licensing Agency, 90 Tottenham Court Road, London W1P 9HE, UK, without the permission in writing of the publisher.

Kruse, John

Debt Recovery in the Court (Wildy Practice Guides series)

British Library Cataloguing in Publication Data

A catalogue record for this book is available from the British Library

ISBN 9780854900732

Typeset in Baskerville MT Pro and Optima LT by Cornubia Press Ltd

Printed and bound in the United Kingdom by Antony Rowe Ltd, Chippenham, Wiltshire

Contents

Preface   xi

1 Preliminaries and Issue of Claims   1
- 1.1 Introduction   1
- 1.2 Limitation of actions   2
- 1.3 Expenses of litigation   3
  - 1.3.1 Court fees   3
  - 1.3.2 Legal costs   3
  - 1.3.3 Disbursements   4
- 1.4 Pre-action protocol and letter before action   5
  - 1.4.1 Pre-action requirements   5
  - 1.4.2 Office of Fair Trading debt collection guidelines   6
- 1.5 Court forms and applications   12
- 1.6 Issue of claims   12
  - 1.6.1 Venue   12
  - 1.6.2 Parties   13
  - 1.6.3 Interest   13
  - 1.6.4 Completing claim forms   14
  - 1.6.5 Issuing claim forms   15
- 1.7 Service of claim forms and documents   16
  - 1.7.1 Address for service   16
  - 1.7.2 Methods of service   18
  - 1.7.3 Certificates of service   21
  - 1.7.4 Failed service   22

2 Responses to Claims and Judgments   25
- 2.1 Introduction   25
- 2.2 Default judgment   25
  - 2.2.1 Conditions   25
  - 2.2.2 Request   26
- 2.3 Admissions   27
  - 2.3.1 Request   28
  - 2.3.2 Determining means   28
  - 2.3.3 Part admissions   30
- 2.4 Defended claims and trials   30
  - 2.4.1 Transfer of claims   31
  - 2.4.2 Allocation questionnaire   31
  - 2.4.3 Stay for settlement   31
  - 2.4.4 Allocation to track   32

vi Contents

		2.4.5	Small claims track	33
		2.4.6	Fast track trials	33
		2.4.7	Multi-track trials	34
		2.4.8	'States paid' defences	34
	2.5	Entering judgment and applications to set aside		34
		2.5.1	The judgment was wrongly entered	35
		2.5.2	There is good reason for setting aside	36
		2.5.3	Claimants have a duty to set aside default judgments	36
3	**Enforcement Preliminaries**			**39**
	3.1	Introduction		39
	3.2	Implications of county court judgments		39
		3.2.1	Registration of judgments	39
		3.2.2	Administration orders	40
	3.3	Enforcement of employment tribunal awards		41
	3.4	Payment of judgments and variations		41
		3.4.1	Receipt of payments	41
		3.4.2	Variation of payments	42
	3.5	Types of enforcement		43
	3.6	Limitations on enforcement		45
	3.7	Information gathering		45
		3.7.1	Application for examination of means	46
		3.7.2	Examination	48
		3.7.3	Adjournment and non-attendance	49
		3.7.4	Suspended orders	49
	3.8	Enforcing a judgment abroad		50
		3.8.1	Enforcement elsewhere in the United Kingdom	50
		3.8.2	Enforcement outside the United Kingdom	51
	3.9	Insolvency		53
		3.9.1	Insolvency as a means of debt recovery	53
		3.9.2	The impact of insolvency on debt recovery	55
		3.9.3	Individual voluntary arrangements	55
		3.9.4	Bankruptcy	56
		3.9.5	County court administration order	57
		3.9.6	Debt relief orders	58
		3.9.7	Company administration orders	58
		3.9.8	Compulsory winding up	59
	3.10	Stays of execution		60
		3.10.1	High Court powers	60

		3.10.2	County court powers	63
		3.10.3	Stays of execution in practice	63
4	**Execution against Goods**			**65**
	4.1	Introduction		65
	4.2	Transfer to the High Court		66
	4.3	Issue of warrants		68
	4.4	Issue and limitations		69
	4.5	Levy process		70
		4.5.1	Notice to debtor	70
		4.5.2	Visits and entry	71
		4.5.3	Levying on goods	71
		4.5.4	Returns and reissues	72
	4.6	Levies against partnerships		73
	4.7	Sale		74
	4.8	Suspension and withdrawal of warrants and writs		75
		4.8.1	Suspension of warrants	75
		4.8.2	Suspension of writs	76
		4.8.3	Withdrawal of warrants	76
	4.9	Interpleader and other claims		77
		4.9.1	County court executions	77
		4.9.2	High Court executions	78
		4.9.3	Exempt goods	79
	4.10	Rent and other claims		79
		4.10.1	Procedure in county courts	80
		4.10.2	Procedure in the High Court	81
		4.10.3	Crown claims	81
	4.11	Negligence by the bailiff		82
5	**Attachment of Earnings Orders**			**85**
	5.1	Introduction		85
	5.2	Application		87
		5.2.1	Definition of earnings	87
		5.2.2	Application procedure	88
		5.2.3	Attachments register	88
	5.3	Disclosure of means		89
		5.3.1	Initial notices	89
		5.3.2	Notices to show cause	90
	5.4	Making orders		90
		5.4.1	Court officers	91
		5.4.2	District judges	91
	5.5	Payment		92
	5.6	Complications		93

		5.6.1 Priority	93
		5.6.2 Suspended orders	94
		5.6.3 Changes in circumstances	94
		5.6.4 Unemployment	94
		5.6.5 Members of the armed forces	95
		5.6.6 Administration orders	95
		5.6.7 Consolidated orders	95
	5.7	Monitoring	96
6	**Third Party Debt Orders**		**99**
	6.1	Introduction	99
	6.2	Attachable debts	99
	6.3	Preconditions	101
	6.4	Application	102
	6.5	Interim order	103
	6.6	Hearing	104
	6.7	Hardship payment orders	106
	6.8	Effect of order and enforcement	106
	6.9	Monies in court	107
7	**Charging Orders and Related Remedies**		**109**
	7.1	Introduction	109
	7.2	Chargeable assets	110
	7.3	Application and interim order	111
	7.4	Hearing	112
	7.5	Effect of order	114
		7.5.1 Land Registry	115
		7.5.2 Other enforcement	115
		7.5.3 Variation or discharge of order	116
	7.6	Orders for sale	117
		7.6.1 Limitations and orders for sale	117
		7.6.2 Application for an order for sale	118
		7.6.3 Application for a possession warrant	119
		7.6.4 Hearing of application	119
		7.6.5 Jointly owned properties	120
		7.6.6 Sale of properties	121
	7.7	Stop orders and notices	122
		7.7.1 Stop notices	122
		7.7.2 Stop orders	123
	7.8	Partnership property	124
	7.9	Receivers by way of equitable execution	124
		7.9.1 Application to court	125
		7.9.2 Appointment by court	126
		7.9.3 Effect of order	127

Appendices				**129**
1	**Prescribed Forms and Precedents**			**129**
	1.1	Letter before action		129
	1.2	Applications for orders for sale		130
	1.3	Stop orders and notices		135
2	**Useful Addresses**			**137**

Preface

Scope of the book

This book aims to offer a simple, practical and realistic guide to the use of the courts for the recovery of debts. It will take readers through the entire process of litigation, from the issue of claims through to the enforcement of judgment debts, outlining the procedure to be followed and giving practical tips at each stage.

The sorts of debts which it is envisaged readers will be seeking to enforce are the following:

- trade debts owed to companies, firms and sole traders;
- personal debts owed between individuals;
- rent arrears due from former tenants and rent unpaid under a money judgment made in conjunction with a possession order; and
- employment tribunal awards.

Awards of damages granted by the courts in other proceedings may also be enforced following the procedures laid down in Chapters 3 to 7.

Jurisdiction of the courts

The county courts and High Court can both potentially deal with the recovery of civil debts, and their procedures are substantially identical due to the progressive the introduction of the Civil Procedure Rules (CPR) since 1998. The CPR and their associated Practice Directions provide a complete code for the conduct of civil litigation and debt recovery in both courts. They will be heavily referred to in the pages that follow. However, it is assumed throughout this text that most claims will be issued in a county court.

CPR, Part 7 states that:

- cases worth less than £15,000 must be commenced in a county court;
- claims worth over £15,000 may be started in either court; but
- trials of disputed claims worth less than £50,000 will be transferred to a county court for hearing.

The clear assumption is that simpler (and smaller) cases should always be dealt with by the county courts, preserving to the High Court higher value, more complex issues. Moreover, statute may restrict certain cases to the county courts alone, for example, the enforcement of employment tribunal awards is a county court matter. Equally, attachment of earnings orders may only be made in a county court, although certain debts may be transferred from a county court to the High Court for enforcement by other means (see Chapter 4). This book will proceed on the assumption that most simple debt litigation will (and should) be a matter for the county courts.

Is court action justifiable?

> As many a claimant has learned to his cost, it is one thing to recover a favourable judgment; it may prove quite another to enforce it against an unscrupulous defendant. But an unenforceable judgment is at best valueless, at worst a source of additional loss. (Lord Bingham of Cornhill in *Société Eram Shipping Co Ltd v Compagnie Internationale de Navigation* [2004] AC 206, para 10, HL)

It is worthwhile considering what ultimately is to be gained by the process, before any litigation is contemplated. Whilst claimants may often wish to see their rights asserted and for justice to be done, it is wise to counsel them upon the costs of this and to be honest with them as to the prospects of getting their money back. Before issuing a claim, a realistic appraisal of how the money might be recovered (and the cost of this) should always be undertaken.

A county court judgment (CCJ) has some value in itself, it is true. It is recorded in a public register and its existence may have some impact upon the defendant's ability to obtain credit in the future. This may be considered by some claimants as justification in itself for taking a person to court. That said, having a CCJ is not the same as having the money. Indeed, it is in some senses quite the opposite, as considerable expense of money, resources and time will have been invested in getting to this point.

I have often met with claimants who are proud possessors of a judgment against the defendant (often after lengthy and difficult disputed proceedings), but it has been my unfortunate duty to advise them that what they have experienced to date is but the beginning of the process. The judgment is merely a piece of paper confirming that they ought to be paid. If the judgment debtor does not feel morally obliged to pay – or does not wish to avoid the registration of the debt by making payment within 30 days of entry of judgment – then it will be necessary to take further court proceedings in order to turn the order to pay into actual hard cash. More expense, more time and more stress will be involved. This being the case, it is sensible to consider whether it is even worth issuing a claim in the first place.

A potential claimant should be advised to weigh up the following issues:

- How much more money are they prepared to commit to the process, given that they are already owed an appreciable amount?
- Given what they already know about the debtor, do they consider that the threat of court proceedings or entry of a judgment will have any tangible effect on the debtor?
- Given what they know about the debtor, if s/he does not settle the judgment promptly, what are the prospects for enforcing it? Chapters 4 to 7 outline the different methods of enforcing CCJs. The creditor needs to consider various key matters – Does the debtor have seizable assets? Does s/he own a property or other chargeable assets? Is s/he working? Does s/he have savings or cash in a bank account?

Below are worked examples that illustrate the potential cost of litigating two different debts, one small and one relatively large. In each case, two different scenarios are envisaged. The debt recovery may proceed smoothly with the debt being admitted and paid in full under a judgment. Alternatively, the debtor may ignore proceedings so that a default judgment must then be enforced – in this example by an examination of means followed by the use of bailiffs – High Court enforcement officers being involved for the larger debt.

Admitted and paid

£5500 owed

- court fees   £225
- legal costs   £155
- total costs   £380

£500 owed

- court fees   £45
- legal costs   £90
- total costs   £135

Ignored and enforced

£5500 owed

- court fees   £425
- legal costs   £211.75
- total costs   £636.75

£500 owed

- court fees   £200
- legal costs   £104.25
- total costs   £304.25

The main point emerging from these examples is the disproportionate cost of enforcing smaller debts. Even where the claim for £500 was admitted and paid, the creditor had to lay out 27% of the debt in advance. In attempts to recover the £500 from the reluctant debtor, costs amounting to 61% of the debt were incurred – and no returns are guaranteed. These figures contrast to 7% and 12% for the larger liability. Plainly, especially careful thought should be given to the advisability of pursuing small debts of hundreds of pounds – although it is important to note that some commercial creditors actively choose to litigate such debts as they consider them more likely to be recovered than sums of thousands of pounds. This is particularly the case if execution on goods is the remedy pursued for non-payment.

It will be apparent from the questions in the third bullet point above that a hierarchy of judgment debtors exists. There are some against whom court proceedings may never be worthwhile – for example, an unemployed individual living in rented, furnished accommodation. An individual in employment may be worth pursuing by attachment of earnings, whilst a homeowner may be pursued by means of a charging order against property they own, but the use of bailiffs to seize domestic chattels may seldom justify the expense. However, if the debtor is a business with shop or factory premises and plant and equipment in their possession, then the use of the bailiff may well be extremely effective.

These questions may discourage a number of clients from taking court action at all. This in turn may appear to encourage default by recalcitrant debtors. Nevertheless, I believe it is important for creditors to be completely realistic about their prospects of success and to consider if their scarce resources could be better employed developing other aspects of their business than in pursuing what may ultimately be a fruitless claim. This is not to deny that some steps should be taken. The debtor should of course be contacted and payment should be demanded (with threats of possible litigation if payment is not forthcoming) but if this fails there will undoubtedly be cases where further action cannot be justified.

1 Preliminaries and Issue of Claims

1.1 Introduction

In this chapter we consider the work that must be undertaken before a claim may be issued and what must be done is initiate a claim for debt in a county court.

The Civil Procedure Rules 1998 (CPR) commence with a statement of the 'overriding objective' of all court proceedings, a set of principles which are used by the courts in the management of cases. The key principles are:

- to ensure that all parties are on an equal footing;
- to save expense;
- to deal with cases in a manner proportionate to the sums of money involved, the complexity of the issues raised, the importance of the cases and the parties' respective financial positions;
- to ensure that all cases are dealt with fairly and expeditiously; and
- to allocate an appropriate share of resources to the management of each case.

The parties to each case have a duty to assist the courts in meeting these objectives. The courts will also be expected to be active in managing cases and in trying to encourage parties to settle cases in order to avoid litigation wherever possible. Key to this is the concept of 'pre-action protocols'. These are a series of steps which parties must follow before any litigation starts so as to ensure full provision of information to each side, clarification of the issues in dispute and the value of the claim and, ultimately, to encourage settlement without the need for the court to be involved. Specific pre-action protocols have been developed for certain specialist kinds of claim; for debts, the general pre-action protocol will apply.

It should be appreciated that claims for undisputed debts, especially those of relatively low value, are low in the list of priorities for county courts. The consequence of this is that they are usually conducted without hearing at most stages of the process. Most decisions on a claim

2 *Preliminaries and Issue of Claims*

will be made by court staff rather than judges and, on the whole, litigation is a paper procedure. This obviously simplifies debt recovery and reduces legal costs for claimants.

1.2 Limitation of actions

In the introduction the issue of the commercial viability of a claim was discussed. Advisers should also consider the legal question of whether or not the claim is statute barred and whether litigation may be begun at all.

Under the Limitation Act 1980 a limitation period of 6 years applies to claims for debt. This period starts to run from the date of default upon the debt – unless it was agreed that the liability was repayable upon demand, in which case the date of the issue of the demand gives rise to the 'cause of action'. Interest likewise runs from the date of default.

Once the limitation period has expired, the debt will be statute barred and the creditor will then be unable to issue a claim in the court, although the debt may still, of course, be pursued by informal means. Provided a claim is issued within the 6-year period, a liability cannot then be barred and no limitation period applies to remedies to enforce judgments (but see para 4.4 on issues of execution).

Fortunately for creditors, a limitation period which has started to run may be re-started by the debtor by either acknowledgment of the debt or part payment, as described below:

- *acknowledgment*: if the debtor provides a written and signed admission of liability to the creditor or his/her agent, this will renew the limitation period. The use of terms such as 'outstanding amount' and 'outstanding balance' in correspondence amount to acknowledgements. A part denial of liability will act as an acknowledgment of the uncontested balance. If a joint debtor makes an acknowledgment of a debt, it is only effective against him/her and not the other debtors.

- *part-payment*: a limitation period may be re-started by a debtor making a payment to a creditor or the creditor's agent in respect of the debt in question. A payment towards interest restarts the limitation period for the capital, but not the interest claimed. Note that, in the case of joint debts, payment by any of the joint debtors restarts the limitation period for all the individuals who are liable. This is in contrast to the consequences of a simple acknowledgment.

Acknowledgment or part payment of a statute-barred debt cannot revive it. In other words, either action by the debtor after the end of the 6-year limitation period cannot restore the creditor's right to take county court action for the liability. Nonetheless, the debtor could not recover such a payment because, as stated, only court action has been barred, not recovery of the debt itself.

1.3 Expenses of litigation

As mentioned in the Introduction, the issue of court action will necessarily increase the debt by the addition of court fees and legal costs. These will be paid up-front by the creditors, before there is any prospect of reimbursement from the debtor, and this consideration must again be weighed in the decision whether or not to start court action. The scale of the potential costs involved was illustrated by the examples in the Introduction.

1.3.1 Court fees

Almost every application to the court involves the payment of court fees. These are noted at the appropriate points throughout the text. The creditor will be liable to pay most of these, whether it is to issue the claim or to initiate enforcement. They become part of the liability and may eventually be recouped from the debtor. Fees may be paid by cash or by cheque or postal order payable to HM Courts Service. Courts cannot take payment by debit or credit card.

It is worth noting, however, that defendants on low pay or benefits may receive remission or reduction of the court fees for which they would otherwise be liable. This may shape their willingness to make applications to court, which for other defendants could pose a significant extra financial burden.

1.3.2 Legal costs

Legal advisers will usually be able to add certain amounts for legal costs to the debts being pursued. The court has discretion in awarding costs, but they are normally allowed to the successful party. In making a decision on this, the court will have regard to the degree of success of the parties and to their conduct – for example, how reasonable it was to pursue a claim and the extent of compliance with pre-action protocols (CPR, Part 44).

The costs applicable to standard debt recovery proceedings will mostly be 'fixed costs' regulated by CPR, Part 45. These apply to the following debt claims – those in which the claim exceeds £25 and the claimant obtained:

4 *Preliminaries and Issue of Claims*

- default judgment;
- judgment on a full or part admission;
- summary judgment; or
- an order that a defence is struck out.

Tables in CPR, Part 45 set out the costs allowed for commencing claims, for entering judgment and for miscellaneous actions such as personal service.

Sample fixed costs allowed by the tables in CPR, Part 45 are as follows:

- *issue of claims*: £50–£110, according to the sum owed. If the defendant pays the sum claimed, including the commencement costs, within 14 days of the service of the particulars of claim, s/he will not be liable for any further costs unless the court orders otherwise;
- *entry of judgment*: £22–£70, depending on the sum due;
- *enforcement costs*, including:
  - £2.25 for the issue of a warrant of execution;
  - £15 per half hour spent at the examination of a debtor;
  - up to £98.50 for the making of a third party debt order; and
  - £110 plus disbursements for the making of a charging order.

All costs become payable 14 days after date of entry of the judgment including them, or after any detailed assessment hearing.

Contested claims allocated to the fast or multi-track attract costs under CPR, Parts 46 and 47. These costs are considerably more extensive and will have to be assessed by the court at the conclusion of proceedings, whether on a summary basis or after a detailed assessment hearing. These costs and procedures will not be discussed in detail here.

1.3.3 Disbursements

Other costs may also be incurred in the course of pursuing a debt. These will include Land Registry fees (see Chapter 7), the cost of reports from credit references agencies or for the use of a tracing agency (see Chapter 3) and the fees of a process server (these will typically charge between £50 and £100 for normal service, but urgent service may attract an hourly rate of £50). Some of these disbursements may be recovered under the order of the court (as when a charging order is made, see para 1.3.2), but others may simply have to be borne by the creditor.

1.4 Pre-action protocol and letter before action

The Ministry of Justice has issued a practice direction dealing with the conduct of parties before any court claim is issued. The aim is to enable disputes to be settled without the need for litigation and to support the efficient management of cases by the courts.

1.4.1 Pre-action requirements

The Ministry of Justice's twin aims for the management of claims are achieved by encouraging parties to exchange information and to consider alternative dispute resolution (ADR) instead of court proceedings. If this practice direction is not complied with, it may have consequences for the conduct of a claim. Parties may be required to explain what steps were taken before court action was commenced where if one party:

- has failed to act within the suggested time limits;
- has failed to supply information;
- has failed to disclose documents; or
- has unreasonably refused to consider ADR;

then sanctions may be imposed. The possible sanctions include suspending the claim until certain steps are taken, the imposition of costs or the deprivation or award of interest to a party as relevant.

Before a claim is issued parties should comply with certain guiding principles. These are:

- to exchange sufficient information about the dispute so that each side may understand the other's position and may make informed decisions about the progress of the case. This will include a properly constituted letter before action and may also require the provision of relevant documents;
- to make appropriate attempts to resolve or settle the dispute;
- to act reasonably and proportionately towards each other, particularly by not imposing high costs on the other side in respect of a relatively low value claim.

In applying these principles, the parties will be expected to take the following actions:

- Claimants should send a letter before action setting out the detail of the dispute (see Appendix 1.1 for an outline of the key contents).

6 Preliminaries and Issue of Claims

- Defendants should make a full written response within a reasonable period of time. In straightforward matters, a reply should be sent in 14 days. In more complex cases, an acknowledgment of the letter before action should be sent within 14 days and a full response should be sent within 30 to 90 days. A longer period for reply than 90 days will only be permitted in very exceptional cases.

- As litigation should be viewed as a last resort, the parties are expected to consider whether some form of ADR, such as mediation, arbitration or simple discussion and negotiation should be attempted first.

If a defendant responds to a letter before action, they may admit the claim in whole or in part or may reject the claim. The defendant should explain the reasons for disputing all or part of a claim and should advise the claimant of any documents upon which they will rely and whether any counterclaim will be made against the defendant. Copies of documents requested should be provided and the defendant may in turn ask for copies of documents from the claimant. The claimant should provide a full response to any counterclaim that is raised, being then in the position of a defendant in that respect. This will oblige the claimant to respond within the time limits laid down in the second bullet point above.

If the letter of action does not produce a response, it can often be helpful to follow this up with a further letter enclosing a copy of the intended claim form. This can offer the other party a last chance to settle or to make contact, backed up by a clear demonstration of the intention to proceed with court action, along with an openness over the exact nature of the forthcoming claim.

1.4.2 Office of Fair Trading debt collection guidelines

The Office of Fair Trading has laid down guidance on good practice in debt collection to which it requires all lenders and debt collection agencies holding a Consumer Credit Act 1974 licence to adhere. Although most readers of this book may not fall into this category, these guidelines on unfair business practices are still worth attention as they indicate best practice in debt recovery.

Communication

It is unfair to communicate, in whatever form, with debtors in an unclear, inaccurate or misleading manner. Examples of unfair practices include:

- use of official looking documents intended or likely to mislead debtors as to their status, such as documents made to resemble court claims;
- leaving out or presenting information in such a way that it creates a false or misleading impression or exploits debtors' lack of knowledge;
- those contacting debtors not making clear who they are, who they work for, what their role is or for what the purpose the contact is being made;
- unnecessary and unhelpful use of legal and technical language, such as use of Latin phrases;
- failing to provide debtors with information on status of debts, for example not providing balance statements when reasonably requested to do so;
- contacting debtors at unreasonable times;
- ignoring or disregarding debtors' legitimate wishes in respect of when and where they should be contacted, for instance, where shift workers ask not to be telephoned during certain times of the day; and
- asking or instructing debtors to make contact on premium rate telephone numbers.

False representation of authority and/or legal position

Those contacting debtors must not be deceitful by misrepresenting their authority and/or the correct legal position. Examples of unfair practices are:

- falsely implying or claiming authority that a person does not possess, such as claiming to work on instructions from the courts or claiming to be bailiffs;
- falsely implying or stating that action can or will be taken when it legally cannot, for instance referring to bankruptcy when the balance is too low to qualify for such proceedings or claiming a right of entry when no court order to this effect has been granted;
- misrepresenting status or backing, such as:
    - using a logo which falsely implies government backing;
    - using a business name which implies public body status; or
    - falsely claiming trade body membership.

8 Preliminaries and Issue of Claims

- falsely implying or stating that action has been taken when it has not, for example that civil action has been taken or that a court judgment has already been obtained;
- falsely implying or stating that failure to pay a debt is a criminal offence or that criminal proceedings will be brought;
- pursuing third parties for payment when they are not liable; or
- taking or threatening to take court action in the wrong jurisdiction, for example taking action against a Scottish debtor in an English court unless legally justified.

Physical/psychological harassment

Putting pressure on debtors or third parties is considered to be oppressive. Examples of such unfair practices include:

- contacting debtors at unreasonable times and at unreasonable intervals;
- pressurising debtors to sell property, to raise funds by further borrowing or to extend their existing borrowing commitments;
- using more than one debt collection business at the same time resulting in repetitive and/or frequent contact by different parties;
- not ensuring that an adequate history of the debt is passed on as appropriate resulting in repetitive and/or frequent contact by different parties;
- not informing the debtor when their case has been passed on to a different debt collector;
- pressurising debtors to pay in full, in unreasonably large instalments, or to increase payments when they are unable to do so;
- making threatening statements or gestures or taking actions which suggest harm to debtors;
- ignoring and/or disregarding claims that debts have been settled or are disputed and continuing to make unjustified demands for payment;
- disclosing or threatening to disclose debt details to third parties unless legally entitled to do so;
- acting in a way likely to be publicly embarrassing to the debtor either deliberately or through a lack of care, for example by failing to put correspondence in a sealed envelope and putting it through a letterbox, thereby running the risk that it could be read by third parties.

Deceptive and/or unfair methods

Dealings with debtors are not to be deceitful and/or unfair. Examples of practices which will violate this principle include:

- sending demands for payment to an individual when it is uncertain that they are the debtor in question, for example threatening debt recovery action against 'the occupier' or sending a payment demand to all people sharing the same name/date of birth as a debtor in the hope that contact with the correct debtor will be made;
- disclosing debt details to an individual when it is uncertain that they are the debtor in question, such as disclosing details to 'the occupier' of an address;
- refusing to deal with appointed or authorised third parties, such as Citizens Advice Bureaux, independent advice centres or money advisers;
- contacting debtors directly and bypassing their appointed representatives;
- operating a policy, without reason, of refusing to negotiate with debt management companies;
- passing on debtor details to debt management companies without the debtors' informed prior consent;
- failing to refer on to the creditor reasonable offers to pay by instalments;
- not passing on payments received to creditors within a reasonable time resulting in delays that adversely affect a debtor's financial position;
- failing to investigate and/or provide details as appropriate, such as when a debt is queried or disputed, possibly resulting in debtors being wrongly pursued;
- requiring an individual to supply information to prove they are not the debtor in question, for example driving licences, passports, full name, date of birth, signatures; and
- not ceasing collection activity whilst investigating a reasonably queried or disputed debt.

Charging for debt collection

Charges should not be levied unfairly. Clearly for legal professionals there is an entitlement to recover certain costs under court orders and the guidance must be read in light of this. However, examples of unfair charges will include:

10 Preliminaries and Issue of Claims

- claiming collection costs from a debtor in the absence of express contractual or other legal provision;
- misleading debtors into believing they are legally liable to pay collection charges when this is not the case, as when there is no contractual provision;
- applying unreasonable charges, that is, charges which are not based on the actual and necessary costs incurred; and
- applying charges which are disproportionate to the main debt.

Debt collection visits

Those visiting debtors must not act in an unclear or threatening manner. Examples of unfair practices are:

- not making the purpose of any proposed visit clear – merely stating that collectors or field agents will call is not sufficient;
- visiting a debtor when it is known they are vulnerable, for instance after a doctor's certificate has been provided stating that the debtor is ill;
- continuing with a visit when it becomes apparent that the debtor is distressed or otherwise vulnerable, for example when it becomes apparent that the debtor has mental health problems;
- entering a property uninvited;
- not leaving a property when asked to do so;
- visiting or threatening to visit debtors without prior agreement when the debt is deadlocked or disputed;
- not giving adequate notice of the time and date of a visit; or
- visiting debtors, unless requested, at inappropriate locations such as at their place of work or at hospital.

Statute-barred debts

This guidance applies to the pursuit of debt regardless of its age. Whilst under the Limitation Act 1980 a recoverable debt may still exist (see para 1.2), the methods by which the debt is collected which may be unfair include:

- pursuing the debt if the debtor has heard nothing from the creditor during the relevant limitation period. If a creditor has been in regular contact with a debtor before the debt is statute barred, it will not be unfair to continue to attempt to recover the debt;

- misleading debtors as to their rights and obligations, for instance by falsely stating or implying that the debt is still legally recoverable and relying on consumers not knowing the relevant legal provisions; and
- continuing to press for payment after a debtor has stated that they will not be paying a debt because it is statute barred. This could amount to harassment contrary to Administration of Justice Act 1970, s 40(1).

Expanding upon the last bullet point above, s 40(1) of the 1970 Act makes it an offence to harass a person in respect of any debt due claimed under contract. Harassment can arise wherever a person:

- harasses another person with demands for payment. which are calculated to subject him or members of his family or household to alarm, distress or humiliation. Demands may constitute harassment because of the frequency with which they are made, the manner or occasion of making any such demand, or any threat or publicity by which any demand is accompanied;
- falsely represents, in relation to the money claimed, that criminal proceedings will lie for failure to pay it;
- falsely represents himself to be authorised in some official capacity to claim or enforce payment; or
- utters a document falsely represented by him to have some official character, or purporting to have some official character which he knows it has not.

A person may be guilty of the offence if he concerts with others in the taking of such actions as are described in the bullets above, notwithstanding that his own course of conduct does not by itself amount to harassment. This will implicate those instructing employees or agents to make visits or phone calls which constitute harassment, even though they do not take any illegal actions themselves.

The Malicious Communications Act 1988 should also be borne in mind in these situations. Section 1 makes it an offence to send any letter or article which conveys a threat or which contains information which is false and which is known, or is believed, to be false by the sender and which the sender knew would be likely to cause distress or anxiety to the recipient. Malicious communications are a criminal offence leading to a fine on summary conviction of up to £2500. It is a defence for the sender of the communication to show that s/he used the threat to reinforce a demand s/he believed there were reasonable grounds for making and that it was believed that the use of the threat was a proper means of reinforcing the demand.

1.5 Court forms and applications

One of the major advantages to county court litigation under the CPR is the comprehensive series of prescribed forms used by the courts. These help to make litigation smooth and simple and save considerable time and expense for all parties. Throughout the book the relevant prescribed and practice forms will be mentioned at the appropriate points. All these forms are available to download from the HM Courts Service website (see Appendix 2).

Of course, the ready availability of forms makes them as accessible to defendants as to creditors and enables the debtor to make a range of applications to the court during the course of litigation and enforcement. The most significant applications which will be encountered repeatedly are:

- *N245*: the application form for reducing an instalment order or suspending a warrant (see Chapters 2, 4 and 5);
- *N244*: the general court application form, which will be mentioned many times, for the purposes of making applications to the court, for example for permission to issue execution outside the limitation period, or to vary the terms of the debtor's payments on a judgment.

For either party to file one of these applications will incur fees. The normal fee for an application on notice on form N244 is £75. Applications made without notice attract a fee of £40 and application on form N245 to vary or suspend will cost the defendant £35.

1.6 Issue of claims

If the debtor does not comply with the final letter before action within the time scale specified, it will be necessary to issue the county court claim. This may be done by the completion of the paper claim forms or it may be done electronically through Money Claim Online (see Appendix 2). Figure 1.1 (see p 23) outlines the process of issuing a claim and obtaining judgment.

1.6.1 Venue

If a paper claim for a debt is to be issued, it may be filed in any county court convenient for the creditor – which may not of course be the court nearest to the debtor. That said, there are number of situations in which the case may be transferred to the debtor's 'home' court. This will be done automatically where:

- the debtor defends the claim;
- the debtor requests a redetermination of a decision by the court;
- a county court district judge (DJ) decides that a request for an instalment order should be dealt with at a hearing; or
- application is made to set aside the judgment.

Automatic transfer only applies in cases where the defendant is an individual. Otherwise an application may be made by a defendant company or firm, arguing that it would be more convenient or fair for the case to dealt with at another court. Transfer will entail extra expense and inconvenience in attending the hearing or appointing a local agent to do so, but it will be a rare occurrence. Most claims are undefended – or often, in fact, are unanswered – so that hearings of any description will seldom take place. Those that do will generally be at the behest of the creditor and will tend to be at the court of issue of the claim.

1.6.2 Parties

This text is written from the perspective of the claimant, the creditor individual, partnership or company. When issuing claims against a defendant debtor, that party's identity requires a little consideration:

- *Partnerships*: partners are jointly and severally liable for debts and two or more persons carrying on business may face a claim in respect of partnership liabilities in the name of the firm in which they traded as partners when the liability accrued. Alternatively, partners may be sued individually rather than under the firm name – but in such cases all partners should then be made defendants. Accordingly, if a claim is issued against only some, they could insist upon the other partners being joined in the claim. That said, an active partner may face a claim alone and may not try to make a sleeping partner liable.
- *Companies*: a company registered under the Companies Acts 1985 and 2006 is a body corporate and may only face a claim in its corporate name. The claim against the company using its corporate title does not need to allege that the company is a corporation or how it was incorporated. Thus, the claim may simply be issued against XYZ Ltd and need not qualify this with words such as 'a company incorporated on 25 October 2009'.

1.6.3 Interest

Over and above the debt which is to be recovered, it is possible for the claimant to recover certain amounts of interest.

A judgment may include a claim for discretionary interest from the date the liability fell due until the date of issue of the claim, and from then until the date of judgment, provided that the statement of claim includes the details required by CPR, r 16.4(2). These are as follows:

- the basis upon which the interest is claimed (whether statutory or contractual);
- the rate and dates for which interest is claimed, including the total amount claimed until the date of calculation (generally the date of issue of the claim) and the daily rate that will accrue thereafter until the date of judgment. The rate must not exceed that allowed by County Courts Act 1981 (CCA 1981), s 69 (8%); and,
- lastly, the request for judgment should include a calculation of the interest claimed for the period between issue of the claim and the date upon which judgment is entered (CPR, r 12.6(1)).

The claim for interest is at the discretion of the court and may be disallowed if there was a long delay in starting proceedings, although the court will make allowance for time spent investigating genuine disputes over liability (see *Adamson v Halifax plc* [2002] EWCA Civ 1134; *Socimer International Bank v Standard Bank* [2006] EWHC 2896 (Comm)). Some claims carry statutory interest from the date of judgment until the date of payment. In all other cases, interest ceases to accrue on judgments after the date upon which judgment is entered. The judgments upon which interest may accrue are those for amounts over £5000 *unless*:

- a payment order allows for a lump sum payment at a later date or payment by instalments. Interest only starts to accrue if payment is not made on the specified date or if an instalment is missed; or
- where an administration order or attachment of earnings order are in place (see Judgments Act 1838, s 17; County Courts (Interest on Judgments) Order 1991 (SI 1991/1184)).

If enforcement proceedings are commenced (other than an application for a charging order), interest will cease to accrue. If no money is recovered, interest starts to accrue again as if no enforcement had been attempted.

1.6.4 Completing claim forms

The claim form required is the Part 7 claim form, practice form N1. The form contains a statement of the nature of the claim, the remedy sought and the value of the claim (CPR, r 16.2). The statement of value should make it clear into which track the claim will fall if it is disputed by the defendant (CPR, r 16.3(2)). This statement of value does not include costs or interest. The particulars of the claim may be entered on the claim form or may be issued as a separate document. In either case the particulars should contain a concise statement of the facts relied upon and the details of any claim for interest which is also being made (CPR, r 16.4). The particulars must be verified by a statement of truth. If separate particulars are to be issued, they must be served upon the defendant within 14 days of the date of issue of the claim, which itself must contain a statement advising the debtor that this document will follow in due course (CPR, r 16.2(2)).

1.6.5 Issuing claim forms

The completed claim form is filed in the court and an issue fee is paid. Currently the scale of fees is based upon the amount claimed. Claims for amounts ranging from a few hundred pounds owed up to £5000 increase in steps for every few hundred or thousand pounds extra demanded. Over £5000 the steps are much larger. For example:

- up to £300 owed – £30
- up to £500 owed – £45
- up to £1000 due – £65
- up to £1500 due – £75
- up to £3000 owed – £85
- up to £5000 owed – £108
- £5000–15000 due – £225

The claim is allocated a unique case number and is served upon the defendant at the address supplied by the claimant on the form. The date of issue of the claim is the date entered upon it by the court (CPR, r 7.2(2). The claimant then has 4 months from the date of issue of the claim form to serve it (see para 1.7).

The claim will be accompanied by four forms known as the 'response pack'. These are:

- *N9*: the acknowledgment of service;
- *N9A*: the admission form;
- *N9B*: the defence and counterclaim; and
- *N9C*: notes for the defendant on completing the forms and responding to the claim.

Form N9 acknowledgement of service is completed by the defendant where either:

- s/he is unable to file a defence within the 14-day time limit allowed by CPR, r 15.4(1)(a); or
- s/he wishes to dispute the court's jurisdiction: this will have to be done by application on form N244 within 14 days (CPR, r 11(4)(a)). If no such application is then made, the defendant will be treated as having accepted that the court has jurisdiction in the claim (CPR, r 11(5)).

Form N9 should be filed in court by the defendant within 14 days of the service of the claim or the service of the particulars of claim if these are served separately from the claim form (CPR, r 10.3). If the defendant wants more time to defend the claim, filing the N9 gives another 28 days from the date of service to do so (CPR, r 15.4(1)(b)). The claimant is notified on form N10 that the acknowledgement of service has been returned to the court.

As mentioned earlier, claim forms may also be issued online. CPR, r 7.12 makes general provision for this and PD 7E provides the detailed rules relating to the Money Claim Online service. If the claim is issued electronically through the Money Claim Online website, the defendant may respond in a similar manner. The acknowledgment of service, part admission and defence may be submitted online.

1.7 Service of claim forms and documents

CPR, Part 6 provides a detailed code for the service of all documents in court proceedings. The rules deal with both claim forms and other documents and, in the main, are identical for both. The term 'claims' includes not only claim forms but any other applications which may be made before proceedings are commenced. For documents other than claim forms, the main differences in procedure are in respect of the address for service and the rules on deemed service, as will be seen.

1.7.1 Address for service

CPR, Part 6 lays down general rules on the address at which claims should be served, but then provides for a number of special cases.

The general rule is that a claim form should be served at:

- the defendant's usual or last known home or business address;
- in the case of claims against partnerships, the partnership's usual or last known business address or the usual or last known residence of each individual partner;

- for limited liability partnerships, the principal office or any place of business having a connection with the claim;
- for corporations, the principal office or any place of business having a connection with the claim; or
- in the case of companies, the registered office or at any place of business of the company which has a real connection with the substance of the claim.

The claim form should include a full address, including postcode, to enable the court to serve the form by post, unless an alternative place or method of service has been ordered. The practice direction to CPR, Part 16 directs litigants to the Royal Mail in order to get a full postcode for the address to be used. PO Box numbers are not acceptable as valid addresses for service. Under CPR, r 6.9 it is made clear that it is the duty of the claimant to make all reasonable efforts to find out the correct address of the defendant. If a current residential or business address cannot be ascertained, the claimant should the give consideration to alternative places and methods of service and should apply to court for permission to use one of these.

A business address has been held not to be an address rented out by the defendant as landlord, even though this may be visited on a regular basis in order to collect rent from the tenants. Nonetheless, there is latitude in the CPR, as the 'usual or last known' address is permitted. If a claim form or document is validly served at such an address, it does not matter that the defendant happens not to be in the country at the time (see *O'Hara v McDougal* [2005] EWCA Civ 1623; *Kamali v City & Country Properties* [2006] EWCA Civ 1879).

The CPR also make provision for a variety of alternative addresses at which service may lawfully be made:

- *a solicitor's business address* may be used if the defendant has provided such an address within England and Wales or if the solicitor has indicated that service will be accepted for the client at that address;
- *a specific address within England and Wales* which the defendant has provided for the purposes of service;
- *for defendants outside England and Wales,* an agent's address within the jurisdiction may be employed where the claim arose within England and Wales and where the agent was involved in that transaction and is still acting for the defendant (CPR, r 6.12);
- *in accordance with a contractual clause* where the contract between the parties makes provision for the place and method of service (CPR, r 6.11);

18 Preliminaries and Issue of Claims

- *where the defendant's current address* cannot be discovered, despite diligent efforts on the part of the claimant, the last known address may be used;

- *where documents are to be served after the commencement of a claim,* different rules are applicable. Under CPR, r 6.23, the defendant is required to supply the court with an address for service for use in the course of the proceedings; this must include a full postcode. The address supplied should be a solicitor's address, a residential or business address or the address of an agent within England and Wales where the party is not based within the country; and

- *for members of the armed forces,* special rules exist under CPR, PD 5 and the annex to that practice direction.

It will be clear that, in some cases, even before any claim may be issued it may be necessary for a potential claimant to incur additional expense discovering or verifying the current address of the intended defendant. This might be dome by means of a credit reference agency search or by use of a tracing agency (see para 3.7).

1.7.2 Methods of service

CPR, Part 6 also makes detailed provision as to *who* may serve claims and documents and *how* they may be served. CPR, r 7.5 lays down a general rule that a claim form must be served by midnight on the calendar day 4 months after the date of its issue. The time for service may be extended under CPR, r 7.6, but application should usually be made by the claimant within the initial 4-month period. If application is made outside this time, the court will only permit an extension if the court has failed to serve the form, or if the claimant can demonstrate that s/he has taken all reasonable steps to serve it and has also acted promptly in making the application to the court when the problems of effecting service became apparent.

The basic rules are as follows. Claim forms and other documents and applications may be served in the following ways:

- *by first class post* or by the use of some other postal carrier which will undertake next day delivery;

- *by document exchange* so long as the correspondence of the defendant or the solicitor includes such an address and there is nothing to indicate that service will not be accepted by such a means;

- *by fax or other means of electronic transmission,* provided that the parties have indicated their prior assent to accept service by such means. A fax or email address included on a letterhead, claim form or statement of case will be sufficient unless use of this number as an address for service has been explicitly contradicted. Service by email may only be upon the legal representative of a party if they have explicitly stated that service by this means is acceptable. Even so, before sending any document by electronic means other than fax, the sender should check whether there are any limitations affecting this methods – for example, the format in which documents should be sent or the size of attachments which may be sent with emails;

- *by leaving documents* at a suitable address; and
- *by personal service* upon the debtor. This will need to be specifically requested by the claimant and can be undertaken by the claimant, his legal representative or a process serving agent. Personal service may take place at any time of day or night but should not be effected on Sunday, Good Friday or Christmas Day without permission. Whoever serves the documents should make efforts first to establish that they are dealing with the correct individual. Service of the documents upon the defendant is then achieved by informing him/her of their contents and by either handing them to him/her or, if s/he refuses to take them, by throwing them down at his/her feet, repeating what they are and that service by this method is valid. The documents should not be enclosed in an envelope, whether sealed or unsealed. Personal service increases the expenses for the claimant, both in terms of legal costs and the fee payable to the process server.

Personal service upon a limited company may be made by leaving the document with any person holding a senior position within the company. CPR, PD 6.2 defines these as:

– *for a registered company or corporation* – a director, treasurer, company secretary, chief executive, manager or other officer; or

– *for any other corporation* – the mayor, chair, president, town clerk or similar officer in addition to those individuals identified above.

County court bailiffs are encouraged to try to make an appointment with a company officer in order to ensure that documents are correctly served. Personal service upon a partnership is effected by leaving the document with a partner or with a person who, at the time of service, has the control or management of the principal place of business of the firm.

In claims against limited companies, forms may also be posted to or left at the company's registered office, addressed to a director or the company secretary. Claims against limited liability partnerships may be served in the same manner under the Limited Liability Partnerships Act 2000 and the regulations made under that statute.

The court will normally serve a claim form unless the claimant has sought permission to do this or a court order or rule of court requires otherwise. In cases of service by the court, service will normally be by first class post (CPR, PD 8).

Alternative methods of service

A claimant may make application under CPR, r 6.15 for permission of the court to serve any claim form or document by a method or at a place different to those so far discussed. Alternative means of service which may be endorsed include service on a relative and service by text. The court will allow this if it is satisfied that there are good reasons to authorise it. It is necessary, therefore, for an application to be supported by evidence of the efforts made to serve the documents so far, the problems encountered and why the proposed alternative method of service is likely to succeed in bringing the claim to the party's attention (see CPR, PD 9). In its order the court will specify the manner of service to be permitted, the date upon which service will be deemed to have taken place and the time periods which will then be allowed to the defendant to respond.

Deemed service

CPR, r 6.14 states that service of a claim form is assumed to have taken place on the second business day after:

- posting the form or leaving it with a delivery service;
- delivering it to or leaving it at an address;
- personal service on the defendant; or
- completion of a fax or email transmission.

Different rules apply to the service of any document issued in proceedings once the claim has been initiated. The date of service is reckoned by business days – these are any day except Saturday, Sunday, bank holidays, Good Friday and Christmas Day. Under CPR, r 6.26 documents are deemed to have arrived at the times set out below:

- by document exchange – on the second business day after it was left with or collected by the provider;
- if faxed, the document will be assumed to have arrived the same day if sent before 4.30 pm. A fax sent after this time is treated as being received the next business day;

- emails will be assumed to have arrived the same day if sent before 4.30 pm. A message sent after this time is treated as being received the next business day; and
- first class post will be assumed to have arrived on the second business day after posting.

CPR, PD 10 provides examples of when deemed service of documents other than claim forms may be assumed. Where the court serves the form, it will notify the claimant when service will be deemed to have taken place. This enables the claimant then to work out when to expect to receive a defence or admission and when it will be possible to apply for a default judgment (see Chapter 2).

In exceptional circumstances, the court has the power under CPR, r 6.16 to dispense with service of a claim form or a document altogether. A claimant may apply for this on form N244 without notice, providing evidence as to why this should be allowed. The guidance to the courts is that dispensing with service should not normally be allowed and that any such application should be approached very strictly. Permission to dispense should only be given in exceptional cases – for example, where there is good evidence to suggest that the defendant is present at an address but is evading service or (conceivably) where the debtor is of no fixed abode (though questions as to whether such a claim is viable and enforceable should also arise in such a situation). In addition, claimants should demonstrate that they have made various attempts to serve the documents by the means allowed by the CPR. Alternatively, service may be dispensed with where the document was served, but where there was some minor and technical irregularity in the process which can be overlooked as the claim has been brought to the other party's attention.

1.7.3 Certificates of service

In any case where the claimant undertakes the service of any documents, it is necessary under CPR, Part 17 for the creditor or his agent to confirm proper service on the defendant by filing in court a certificate of service on form N215. This should be done within 21 days of service of the particulars of claim, unless all defendants have submitted acknowledgments of service within that time. Default judgment may not be obtained unless a certificate has been filed.

The certificate details the date of posting, leaving or transmitting the claim form. For the service of documents (as opposed to claims), a time of service must also be included (CPR, r 6.29). This is for the purpose of ascertaining the date of deemed service as described in the previous section. There is no need to file in court with the certificate copies of any documents already in the court's possession.

Where the county court bailiff has been required to serve documents, a certificate of service will also be completed for the court records. This will confirm how service was effected or, if attempts to serve the documents were unsuccessful, what obstacles were encountered – which may assist the claimant is choosing an alternative means of service to try.

1.7.4 Failed service

It is assumed that a claim form has been served unless the claimant has failed to supply an address as allowed by the court rules (see para 1.7.1). However, in some cases it will become apparent that service has failed. Where the court serves a claim form by post and it is returned to the court by Royal Mail, the court will send the claimant notice. Similarly the court will notify the claimant if the county court bailiff has been unable to serve the form. In such cases the court is under no obligation to try to serve the document again and it will be for the claimant to undertake further investigations to confirm the address, or find an alternative address, before attempting some other means of service themselves.

Preliminaries and Issue of Claims 23

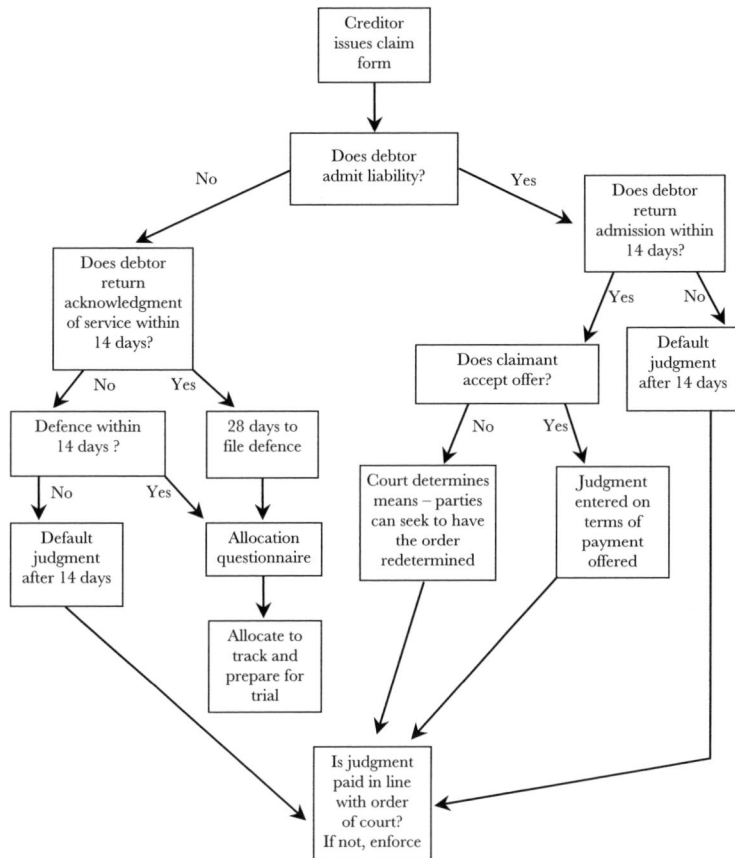

Figure 1.1: Debt claims – issue to judgment

2 Responses to Claims and Judgments

2.1 Introduction

This chapter guides readers through the process of dealing with the defendant's response to the claim. The handling of disputed claims is outlined, but is not be considered in detail, and the chapter concludes with the entry of judgment against the debtor and examines the possibility of a later application seeking to overturn this judgment. Figure 1.1 (see p 23) outlines the process of issuing a claim and obtaining judgment.

2.2 Default judgment

A default judgment may be entered where a defendant has failed to respond to the claim: that is, where s/he has not filed an acknowledgment of service nor a defence, so there has been no trial of the claim, nor has there been an admission of liability (CPR, r 12.1).

2.2.1 Conditions

CPR, r 12.3 sets out the exact conditions to be satisfied to entitle a claimant to enter a default judgment. This right may arise in three situations:

- *Acknowledgment of service*: judgment may be obtained in default of an acknowledgment of service only if:
    - the defendant has not filed an acknowledgment (N9), or a defence (N9B), or any part of such a document; and
    - the time for doing so (14 days) has expired.
- *Defences*: a claimant may only obtain a judgment in default of a full defence of the claim where:
    - the defendant filed an acknowledgment of service but failed then to file a defence; and
    - the time for doing so (14 days) has expired.

Of course, situations will arise where the defendant submits a defence to the court *after* the time limit for doing so but *before* a default judgment has been entered. Strictly speaking, the claimant is entitled to insist upon a default judgment at this point, but the court may permit the defendant to also submit an application for an extension of time and may accept the defence provided a good case against the claim can be shown (see *Coll v Tatum* [2001] 3 *LS Gazette Reports* 26).

- *Admissions*: if the defendant fails to file an admission form in response to the claim, identical principles will apply. A claimant may not obtain a default judgment if:

    – there is a pending application by the defendant for summary judgment under CPR, Part 24. This might be made where it is argued that there is no substantive claim to answer, or that issue of the claim consitutes an abuse of process on the part of the claimant;

    – the defendant has satisfied the claim in full, including costs; or

    – in a claim for money, the defendant has filed an admission under CPR, r 14.4 or r 14.7 with a request for time to pay, even though this was filed outside the time limit of 14 days set in the CPR (CPR, r 12.3).

Acknowledgments and defences are filed in the court. Admissions and offers of payment are sent to the claimant or his/her agent by the defendant. It is important, therefore, carefully to monitor the progress of such claims. Once the period of 14 days has passed from the date of service (which will be specified by the court) and provided that no admission has been received, nor has notice of any defence or intended defence been received from the court, the claimant will be in a position to make an immediate request for judgment.

2.2.2 Request

To obtain a default judgment the claimant must file a request on form N205 (CPR, r 12.4). This may, under CPR, r 12.5, specify the date by which the whole judgment debt should be paid (either forthwith or by a single lump sum payment within 14 or 28 days) or the times and rate by which it may be paid by instalments. It is fair to say that, at this stage, many creditors will seek for a 'forthwith' judgment ordering the debtor to make full payment immediately, thus enabling enforcement to be initiated straight away. Depending on the nature of the debt and the circumstances of the debtor, this may be appropriate, but it will necessarily involve further outlay in fees and costs for the creditor. In some cases, especially where the debtor is known to be an individual whose income may be low and received periodically, it may be more prudent to stipulate a realistic level of instalment payment.

The judgment will be entered for the amount of the claim (including any interest claimed but less any payments which have been made since issue) plus all costs and fees to be paid. A payment order will be made requiring discharge of the debt at the rate and by the date(s) specified in the request or, if none is specified, immediately (CPR, r 12.5(2)).

CPR, Part 12, PD 4.1 requires that a request for a default judgment should be accompanied by the evidence that the defendant is entitled to a default judgment. This will comprise the following evidence:

- that the statement of claim has been served upon the defendant (a certificate of service on the court file will be sufficient evidence of this);
- that the defendant has not served an acknowledgment of service nor a defence;
- that the time for such a response has passed; and
- that the defendant has neither satisfied the claim nor filed an admission under CPR, r 14.4 or r 14.6.

The court will then draw up the default judgment on form N30 and will serve it on the defendant, who must comply with the terms of payment or face enforcement. If 6 months elapse from the end of the period allowed for the filing of a defence and no defence or admission has been filed – nor has a default judgment or summary judgment been entered by the claimant – a claim will be automatically stayed under CPR, r 15.11(1). It would then be necessary for one of the parties to apply under CPR, r 15.11(2) for permission to lift the stay. The application would be on form N244 and should give reasons for the applicant's delay in proceeding with or responding to the claim (CPR, Part 15, PD 3.4).

2.3 Admissions

Under CPR, r 14.1(1) it is possible for a defendant to admit the truth of all or part of a claimant's claim. This may be done by giving notice in writing, by statement of claim or by letter (CPR, r 14.1(2)), or, where a claim is solely for the payment of money, by making an admission under either CPR, r 14.4 (an admission of the full amount claimed) or under r 14.5 (an admission of part of the amount claimed) on the practice form supplied (N9A).

The CPR allow for a situation where a written admission is made before proceedings have been commenced (CPR, r 14.1(A)(1)) but it will usually be received after the issue of the claim form. An admission should be filed by the defendant within 14 days of the service of the particulars of claim (if these have been served separately) or, in any other case, within 14 days of service of the claim form (CPR, r 14.2(1)). An admission may be filed late provided that no default judgment has been entered (CPR, r 14.2(3)). Part 14 will still apply to such late admissions.

Even though an admission has been filed, it is possible for a defendant to seek permission of court under CPR, r 14.5 to later withdraw it. For this to be allowed by the court, it will have to be convinced that it is generally in the interests of justice to allow it. The court will take a number of factors into account when considering such an application:

- the grounds for the request – for example, has new evidence come to light altering the defendant's assessment of their position?
- the conduct of both parties in the matter;
- the prejudice to each side that will arise as a result of granting or refusing permission; and
- the prospects of success on either side.

2.3.1 Request

The normal procedure in debt claims will be for the defendant to admit the claim by completing reply form N9A and sending it directly to the claimant. If the whole claim is admitted, the claimant may then simply enter judgment by filing form N30(1) with the court. If the defendant has not requested time to pay on the admission form, the claimant may specify the manner of payment – the date by which full payment should be made or the dates and rate of instalment payments. Judgment for the balance and interest and costs may then be entered by the claimant (CPR, r 14.4).

2.3.2 Determining means

If the defendant in his/her admission seeks time to pay the sum claimed (whether by proposing instalments or a later date for payment in full) acceptance of this offer may be made by the claimant when applying for judgment. This application is made on form N225 (CPR, r 14.9(4)) and judgment will be for the balance of the claim plus costs and interest coupled with an order for payment at whatever rate or time the defendant has proposed and the claimant has accepted.

If the defendant seeks time to pay the debt but the claimant does not agree to the offer (either the level of payments or the suggestion of instalment payments), notice of this must be filed with the request for judgment, including a copy of the admission form (CPR, r 14.10). The creditor must give the court reasons why the offer of payment is rejected – for example, by pointing out any inaccuracies or inconsistencies there may be in the information provided by the defendant. The court will then determine the rate of payment before entering judgment on form N30(2). Determinations will take into account the defendant's statement of means, the claimant's objections as set out on the form N225A and 'any other relevant factors' (CPR, Part 14, PD 5.1). For a claim of up to £50,000 the determination of means is carried out by a court officer without a hearing (CPR, r 14.11). HM Courts Service has provided guidance to court staff on the conduct of determinations. The guiding principles to be applied in this process are common sense and reasonableness. Over and above the defendant's expenditure on housing and utility costs and regular food expenses, allowance will be made essentials such as childminding costs, travel to work expenses and other expenses not specifically allowed for in form N9A, whilst 'frivolous' or 'non-essential' items of expenditure such as pocket money and money for entertainment will be disallowed (although a £15 per week sundries allowance is permissible).

The figures determined by the court officer are transferred to a standard form (EX120), the determination of means calculator. On analysing this, there may be four conclusions:

- the debtor's disposable income exceeds the sum offered but is less than the figure requested by the creditor. The court should order payment of the amount of the disposable income;
- the debtor's disposable income exceeds the sum requested by the creditor. The court should order payment of the amount the creditor requested;
- the debtor's disposable income is lower than the sum offered. The court should order payment of the amount offered unless this seems 'unreasonably high'; and
- the debtor's disposable income is calculated to be a nil or negative figure, in which case the court should order payment of the amount offered by the defendant unless this seems 'unreasonably high'.

If the standard form N9A is examined, it will be noted that it is designed to be applicable to individual debtors and does not accommodate self-employed persons, partnerships or companies. This will make it difficult for the court officer to apply HM Courts Service guidelines and in such cases the matter is likely to be referred to a judge for determination.

A judge may determine the payment for higher claims, without a hearing if necessary (CPR, r 14.12(1)). If a hearing is considered to be necessary the case will be transferred to the defendant's home court (CPR, r 14.12(2)). When conducting a determination, there is no obligation for a judge to follow the guidelines or principles applicable to court staff.

Any determination may be challenged subsequently by either party. No court fee is payable for such a request. This 're-determination' will be performed without hearing by a judge if the initial determination was by a court officer, although it is possible for the party making the application to ask at the same time that the matter be dealt with at a hearing. If the original determination was by a judge a reconsideration will be at a hearing before a judge – unless the parties agree otherwise (CPR, Part 14, PDs 5.4 and 5.5). Application for this should be made on form N244 within 14 days of service of the notice of determination (CPR, r 14.13).

2.3.3 Part admissions

If a part admission is made by the defendant by filing N9A in court the claimant will be notified by the court and s/he will be required to respond on form N225A indicating which if the following three responses applies:

- whether the part admission is accepted in satisfaction of the claim;
- whether the offer is rejected and the claim should continue; or
- whether the part admission (but not the proposals for payment) is accepted.

The claimant should respond within 14 days and a copy of this should be served upon the defendant by the court (CPR, r 14.5(4)). The claim is stayed until a reply is filed if none is received from the claimant within the 14-day period (CPR, r 14.5(5)). Requests for time to pay and for entry of judgment are handled as described above.

2.4 Defended claims and trials

If the defendant wishes to contest the case, a defence must be filed in court on form N9B within 14 days of the service of the particulars of claim or, if an acknowledgment of service was filed, within 28 days of service of the particulars (CPR, r 15.4(1)). The parties may agree to allow an extra 28 days for a defence to be filed (CPR, r 15.6) and in such cases the defendant must notify the court of this. Form N9B allows for a counterclaim also to be made against the claimant under CPR, Part 20. It is possible also to make a part admission of a claim, accepting liability for part of the sum claimed but defending liability for the balance; this is done by filing both admission *and* defence forms with the issuing court.

2.4.1 Transfer of claims

Defended cases may be transferred to another court for trial. If the proceedings are for a specified sum of money, if the claim was commenced in a court which is not the court most local to the defendant and if the defendant is an individual, then when a defence is filed the case will automatically be transferred to the defendant's 'home court' (CPR, r 26.2).

2.4.2 Allocation questionnaire

Following the receipt of a defence at the court, an allocation questionnaire (AQ) (form N149 for small claims case and N150 for cases valued at over £5000) will be sent by the court to each party for completion. The claimant pays a fee for filing this. For small claims cases the fee is £35 if the claim is for more than £1,500; in all other cases involving sums over £5000, a fee of £200 is payable. A date is specified for the return of the AQ by both parties, which will be at least 14 days after the date of its service. When filing the AQ a party may also file extra information which it is considered will assist the court in the management of the case, such as notice of an intention to issue a counterclaim or a list of directions which it is believed are necessary to the case. This will enable the court to deal with as many aspects of the case at one hearing as possible. It is expected that parties should consult on the completion of their AQs. If a party fails to file an AQ, the court may give whatever directions it considers appropriate, for example, ordering that a claim be struck out.

2.4.3 Stay for settlement

At the time of filing the AQ a party can request that a stay is imposed upon the claim to enable the claim to be settled, whether by negotiation, ADR or by some other method. Where parties request this or where the court considers it to be appropriate, the claim may be stayed for one month (CPR, r 26.4). A stay may be extended for up to another month, but the court will have to be satisfied that extra time is worthwhile and that a settlement is in prospect. It is the duty of the claimant, within 14 days of the end of the period of the stay, to notify the court of the outcome of the delay – whether or not a settlement has been reached. If no such notice is received, the court will give case management directions.

2.4.4 Allocation to track

The defended case will then be allocated to one of three tracks and preparations for hearing of the disputed claim will begin (CPR, r 26.5). Further information may be sought from the parties by the court on form N15 (CPR, r 26.6) or a hearing may be arranged in order to obtain this, in which case notice is served on form N153. The scope of each track is as follows:

- *Small claims track*: this track is for personal injury and housing disrepair cases valued up to £1000 and for all other claims up to a value of £5000. The simpler procedure of this track is intended to be proportionate for straightforward disputes over relatively small sums.
- *Fast track*: this track is for any claim which is not a small claim and which is worth no more than £15,000 – unless the court considers that the trial of the claim will last longer than one day and that oral evidence from more than one expert witness or in more than two separate fields of expertise per party will be required.
- *Multi-track*: this is for any other claim and such cases will normally be transferred to the local county court trial centre.

In allocating a case the court will have regard to a number of factors. These will include:

- the value of the claim;
- the complexity of the law, facts or evidence involved;
- the number of parties;
- the value of any counterclaim;
- the amount of oral evidence to be heard; and
- the circumstances of the parties.

Cases cannot be allocated to a track for which a claim's value is too high unless the parties consent (CPR, r 26.7(3)).

Once the allocation decision has been made, notice is served upon the parties with copies of the other side's AQ and any further information that was filed at the same time as the AQ. A case can be reallocated if necessary, on application from a party. This might be done where a relatively straightforward dispute has been allocated to a more complex track than is necessary or (more likely) where it is felt that the trial of the case is likely to be longer and more complex, in terms of evidence, that the court has anticipated.

2.4.5 Small claims track

Standard directions for the hearing of the case will be issued at least 21 days in advance of the hearing date, requiring the parties to serve or file any documents to be relied upon at the hearing. Permission of court is required if oral or written expert evidence will be used at the trial. If all parties agree, there need not be an actual hearing of the case (CPR, r 27.10). A further fee for the pre-trial checklist and the setting of the hearing date is payable in advance of the hearing – for small claims this is between £25 and £300 depending on the amount claimed. This fee may be refunded if the case is settled within at least 7 days of the hearing date.

There are two key aspects to the small claims track. The first is that the legal costs that may be recovered from the losing party are extremely limited (CPR, r 27.14 and PDs 7.1 to 7.3). This is of considerable significance to a claimant. If there is any likelihood that a claim for a small debt will be challenged, it may not be worthwhile incurring the costs of legal representation throughout the process as the court will seldom permit these to be added to and recovered as part of the debt. The second significant point is that the rights of appeal against small claims decisions are very restricted. An appeal to circuit judge is only possible where there has been a mistake in law or 'a serious irregularity affecting the proceedings'. As a result, in most cases an appeal will not be possible. This at least has the advantage of limiting litigation and capping further expenses for a claimant. Given these restrictions, where a smaller claim is disputed and is allocated to the small claims track, it will often be sensible for the claimant to consider whether a settlement with the defendant is worthwhile. Although this may involve recovery of less than the full amount claimed, this reduced recovery is offset by the saving of time and expenses. Preparing for and attending a small claims hearing will involve an appreciable commitment of time and resources and in most cases this outlay must be borne by the claimant even if the defence fails and is dismissed.

2.4.6 Fast track trials

Cases on this track are governed by CPR, Part 28. When allocating a case to the fast track the court will give standard directions for its management and a timetable for the steps leading up the trial. A trial date will be set, or a period of 3 weeks will be specified within which it will take place, there being a maximum period of 30 weeks between the issue of the directions and the date of the trial. The directions cover such issues as disclosure and inspection of documents, expert evidence and witness statements.

2.4.7 Multi-track trials

These cases are covered by CPR, Part 29. When allocating a case to the track the court may set a timetable and give directions or it may arrange a pre-trial review hearing or case management conference. Case management in multi-track cases will be flexible to the nature of the case and the parties will be expected to co-operate in preparing the matter for hearing at trial.

For both fast track and multi-track cases the legal costs of preparing for and attending trial will potentially be substantial. In addition, the court will require further significant fees. When the pre-trial checklist is issued, a fee of £100 is payable for fast track cases and £1000 for multi-track. Setting the trial date incurs a further fee of £500 or £1000 respectively, although settlement before the trial can attract a percentage refund of these sums depending upon how much notice is given to the court.

2.4.8 'States paid' defences

There is a special category of defence previously known as 'states paid' and now termed 'money claimed has been paid' under CPR, r 15.10. Where the only claim is for money and the defendant states in his/her defence that the sum has already been paid in full, the court serves notice of this on the claimant on form N236. This requires the claimant to respond stating whether or not s/he wishes the claim to proceed. The claimant has 28 days in which to do this and must also serve a copy of the response on the defendant (CPR, r 15.10(2)). If the claimant fails to respond within 28 days of the service of the notice, the proceedings on the claim will be stayed under CPR, r 15.10(3). An application on notice in N244 will then be necessary to lift the stay; either party is entitled to apply. The applicant would have to explain in this the reasons for the delay in responding to the court and in proceeding with the claim (CPR, Part 15, PD 3.4).

In such instances, if the claimant asks that the proceedings continue, the case will be allocated to the appropriate track as described. If the claimant responds to the court stating that s/he does not wish to proceed with the claim, the court will close its case file.

2.5 Entering judgment and applications to set aside

The county courts will prepare and serve all judgments and orders (CPR, r 40.3). A party must comply with a judgment within 14 days unless:

- a different date for compliance is given;
- payment by instalments has been ordered (see further discussion of this at para 3.4);
- a different date is given in the CPR; or
- the court has stayed the proceedings or the judgment.

Claimants should be aware that proceedings might be stayed for two reasons:

- because the defendant has appealed the decision. The court may impose a stay in special cases, but the mere existence of a challenge to the judgment is not reason enough alone to prevent execution; or
- because the defendant has made an application on the grounds that s/he is unable for some reason to comply with the court's order. This is the situation far more likely to be encountered by judgment creditors in the run of things.

Both of these issues are examined in detail at para 3.10.

In most cases though, once judgment has been entered in a case and an order for payment has been made, it will appear that the case has moved from the second to the third stage of the recovery process and that the claimant is now in a position either to collect payment or to enforce the judgment. Nonetheless, claimants should be prepared for situations in which the defendant seeks to reverse the situation and to set aside the judgment.

Where a judgment is entered in default, it is possible for the defendant to apply to the court to have it set aside under CPR, Part 13. There are three situations in which the court may exercise its discretion to set aside a default judgment. In all cases, application will be made by the defendant on form N244. A court fee of £75 is payable, which may discourage the more frivolous applications, and a hearing date will be arranged.

2.5.1 The judgment was wrongly entered

An application to set aside may be made where the correct procedure laid down in the CPR has not been followed. The defendant may allege that the claim had been satisfied in full or that an acknowledgment of service or a defence had been filed or the time for doing so had not expired when the claimant applied for judgment (CPR, r 13.2)).

2.5.2 There is good reason for setting aside

An application to set aside will be possible where the defendant is able to demonstrate a real prospect of successfully defending the claim and can also show that there are other good reasons why the judgment should be set aside so that the s/he may have the opportunity to defend it (CPR, r 13.3(1)).

In considering whether to set aside, the court must consider whether the defendant applied promptly once s/he knew of the existence of the judgment. Delay on the part of the defendant need not be for a very long period. An application made after 28 days has been held to be too late, whilst an application after 30 days, the delay being explained by the need to seek legal representation, was at the very limits of acceptability (see *Regency Rolls Ltd v Carnall* [2001] All ER (D) 1417; *BCCI v Zafar* [2001] All ER (D) R 21). If there is delay and if it also appears that the main motive behind the application was to frustrate recovery of the judgment debt, it will be regarded as an abuse of process and the application will be refused (see *Nolan v Devonport* [2006] EWHC 2025 (QB)).

A request to set aside judgment might be made where the claim went astray or was delayed in the post, where the address for service was no longer a current address for the defendant or where, for some other reason (such as illness or absence from home) the person was unable to deal with the matter in time. The mere fact that a claim form was not received is, on its own, not a reason for setting aside. If the claim is admitted, there is no point cancelling the judgment merely to reinstate it once again. The court will need to be convinced that there are genuine grounds for contesting the claim as well as genuine reasons for not acting within the proper time. Nonetheless, the court has said that, if the claim was never served by the claimant or was never served by the method claimed, a judgment should always be set aside, regardless of the defence. This will at least permit the defendant who admits the debt to settle without incurring more than the commencement costs (see *Credit Agricole Indosuez v Unicof Ltd* [2002] EWHC 77 (Comm)).

2.5.3 Claimants have a duty to set aside default judgments

If the claimant later has 'good reason to believe' that the particulars of claim did not reach the defendant before the judgment was entered (CPR, r 13.5). In such cases the claimant must file a request for the judgment to be set aside, or should apply to the court for directions, and may take no further steps to enforce the judgment until the matter has been determined. This situation is most likely to arise because it is possible to serve documents at the 'last known' residence or place of business of the defendant. Subsequent contact from the debtor or information discovered whilst preparing to enforce a judgment might reveal that the address for service used was incorrect or out of date.

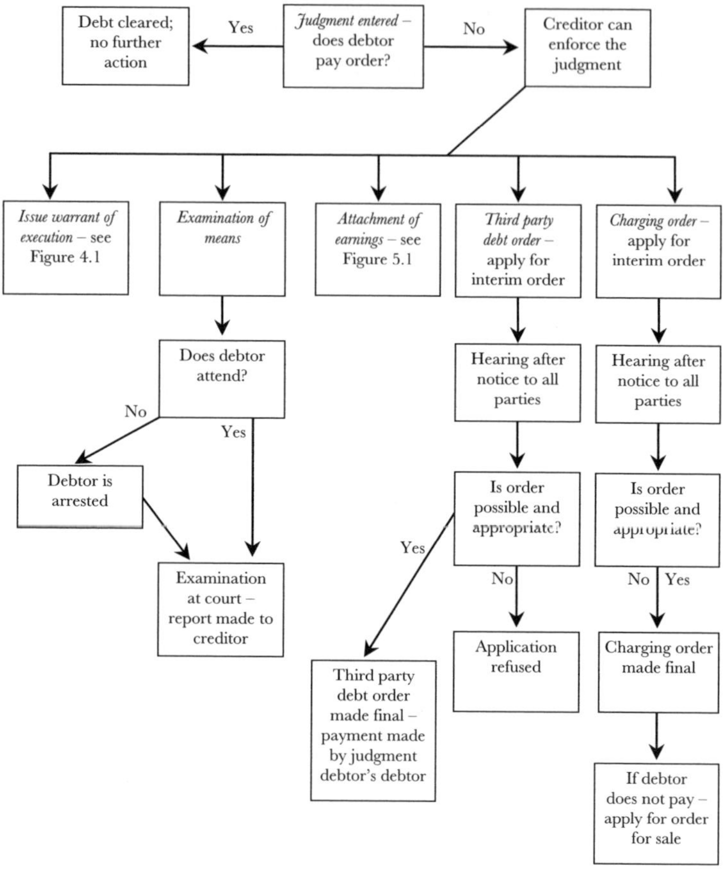

38 *Responses to Claims and Judgments*

Figure 2.1: Enforcement of judgments

3 Enforcement Preliminaries

3.1 Introduction

This chapter examines the further work that must be undertaken before enforcement of a judgment can be commenced effectively. Figure 2.1 (see p 38) outlines the different procedures for enforcing a judgment. The first stage is for the circumstances of the judgment debtor to be discovered and analysed and for the best means of enforcement to be matched to that information.

A number of related issues are also considered. A tribunal award may be registered as a county court order and enforced in the same manner as a judgment; this process is outlined. Three aspects of insolvency are also discussed – bankruptcy and winding-up are mentioned as a possible means of enforcement; the consequences of the debtor's insolvency on recovery are considered. In particular, county court administration orders are outlined, as they may be founded upon the creditor's judgment debt.

3.2 Implications of county court judgments

The making of a county court judgment (CCJ) against a debtor has a number of implications, both positive and negative for the creditor. These are as follows:

- a payment order will be made at the same time. The judgment debtor will be under an obligation to comply and will face enforcement of the judgment if s/he does not pay;
- the CCJ will be registered and may effect the person's ability to get credit in the future (see para 3.2.1); and
- the debtor will be able to apply for an administration order.

3.2.1 Registration of judgments

A CCJ is registered against a debtor's name with the Register of Judgments, Orders and Fines. The information on the register will in turn be recorded by credit reference agencies.

Records of judgments are kept by the Register and by reference agencies for up to 6 years. Even if a judgment is cleared in full during this period, this will only lead to the files being amended accordingly – the record of the initial judgment will remain. However, if the judgment debt is satisfied in full within 30 days of entry of judgment, the record will be cancelled by Register.

3.2.2 Administration orders

Once a judgment has been entered against an individual, it may actually enable them to ameliorate their financial situation. This statement may sound counter intuitive, but where a person has at least one CCJ outstanding in his/her name and has debts of less than £5000, s/he can apply to a county court for an administration order to be made.

An administration order consolidates all the outstanding accounts for which the person is liable into one order which is administered by the court. The debtor will be required to make a monthly payment towards the consolidated debts, the level of this instalment being set in light of the person's means. The application form N92 incorporates a statement of means along with a list of all outstanding debts and judgments. Creditors are served with notice of an application and are entitled to object to their inclusion on the order. DJs are generally sympathetic to requests for exclusion from statutory or priority creditors, such as landlords or local authorities recovering council tax, but it is much less likely that an ordinary personal debt will be excluded unless there are some very unusual circumstances surrounding it. Once scheduled to an order, the creditor is bound by it. The only means of obtaining payment will be through the court under the terms of the administration order and any further independent recovery action will be next to impossible. The impact of the order upon ongoing enforcement is discussed at para 3.9.

No fee is paid by the debtor upon filing a request for an administration order. However, the court deducts 10 pence in the pound from the payments received to cover its administrative costs. Whilst the maximum debt level for orders is admittedly low and the number of orders made each year is also low, they can clearly be of great value to certain indebted individuals. Administration orders are equally of very little benefit to judgment creditors; they are a risk of debt litigation (albeit a rare one) and, it should also be mentioned, once an order is in place, it will be found that payments will tend to be made rather infrequently by the court office. If the person does not make payments as ordered, the order will be revoked.

3.3 Enforcement of employment tribunal awards

The award of an employment tribunal may be enforced through the county court as if it was an order of that court. Application is made to the court for the district where the defendant resides or carries on business under CPR, r 70.5.

The application is made without notice to the defendant on form N322A; a fee of £35 is payable. This application requires the claimant to provide the court with the details of the person subject to the order and the balance remaining unpaid under the award. A copy of the tribunal decision should be filed with the application form. The request will be dealt with by a court officer, who will register the award as an order of the court so that it may be enforced by all the means to be described in this chapter and subsequently. Under CPR, r 45.6 fixed costs of between £30.75 and £75.50 may also be added, according to the size of the sum due under the award.

Provided that the application satisfies the requirements of CPR, r 70.5 the court cannot refuse to register the order. It does not have the power to investigate the grounds for the tribunal award and cannot entertain any appeal on this basis. If the defendant wishes to challenge the decision, this should be done before the tribunal (see *Ghassemian v LB Kensington & Chelsea* [2009] EWCA Civ 743).

3.4 Payment of judgments and variations

In most cases, the court does not handle payments received from a judgment debtor. Money will normally only be transmitted via the court in two situations – where an attachment of earnings order has been made and where an administration order is in place. It is also unusual, in ordinary debt cases, for the court to review either the regularity or level of payment by the debtor. That said, it is certainly possible for the court to make such an order on application at the hearing.

3.4.1 Receipt of payments

In most cases, it will be necessary for the creditor or his legal representative to make arrangements with judgment debtors for them to make payments to them – whether by lump sum or instalments. Where the court order allows for periodical payments, the creditor should monitor compliance with the court order and will accordingly be well placed to follow up and to enforce payment whenever default takes place.

3.4.2 Variation of payments

Even after the entry of a judgment the parties may still apply to the court for a variation of the terms of the judgment. This may be done under CPR, Part 14, PD 6.1 where 'on account of a change in circumstances since the date of the decision (or redetermination, as the case may be)'. Application may be made to vary the time and rate of the instalments remaining to be paid on the judgment debt.

These applications are most likely to be made by defendants in situations where their financial circumstances have changed for the worse (for example, redundancy or birth of a child). The application is made on form N245, setting out the person's income and expenditure. A fee of £35 is payable. The claimant will be notified of this on form N246 and has the choice whether to accept or refuse the revised offer of payment. If it is rejected by the claimant, the court will follow the determination procedure described in para 2.3 in respect of admitted claims.

It is, however, possible for a claimant to make an application for variation of the payment where it is believed that the debtor's situation has improved and a higher repayment is now possible. Under CPR, Sch 2: County Court Rules (CCR), Ord 22, r 10(2) the application may be either to substitute an instalment order or smaller instalments or a later date for a lump sum payment. The claimant submits form N294 to the court and normally the court will vary payment as requested, unless no payment at all has been made, in which case the matter is referred to a DJ. Under CCR, Ord 22, r 10(3) application may be made by the claimant for a lump sum payment sooner than had been ordered, for a lump sum order to replace an instalment order or for higher instalments. These applications are automatically passed to the debtor's home court for hearing before a DJ. Such requests are often made by commercial creditors as a means of precipitating default and thereby permitting enforcement (see para 7.4).

Situations may arise where the judgment debtor makes payment on a CCJ after the creditor has submitted an application for enforcement of the judgment to the court, or after the court has issued execution upon the judgment. Where this happens, it is the duty of the creditor to immediately notify the court or, if appropriate the High Court enforcement officer (HCEO), of the payment that has been received (CPR, Part 70, PD 7.1).

3.5 Types of enforcement

All forms of enforcement in county courts are technically termed 'execution', but use of the word is usually limited to the process of enforcement by means of seizure of the judgment debtor's goods under a warrant of execution. There are a number of forms of enforcement available in county courts and the High Court for the recovery of an unpaid judgment debt. These are briefly outlined and assessed at this point. The creditor may choose from:

- *warrant of execution* against the goods and chattels of the debtor;
- *attachment of earnings order* against the wages or salary of the debtor;
- *third party debt order* against the bank account, savings or debts of the individual; or
- *charging order* against the property of the debtor.

A judgment creditor may use more than one of these methods of enforcement, either at the same time or sequentially (CPR, r 70.2(2)(b)).

It is also possible to apply for examination of the debtor in court. This is not really a form of enforcement, rather it is an adjunct or preliminary to enforcement and as such is discussed below.

As suggested in the Introduction, even before a claim is issued it may be sensible to consider how any subsequent judgment might be effectively enforced against the debtor in order to determine whether court action is worthwhile. Certainly at the point of entering judgment, it will become imperative to address this question. Paragraph 3.1 outlines the implications for the debtor of a CCJ being registered. For some creditors this may be compensation enough. However, if the hope is to turn the court order into money, then the pros and cons of each form of enforcement must be weighed up. Table 3.1 outlines these issues.

It is also possible to enforce the judgment by means of the issue of some form of insolvency proceedings. This issue is explored in detail at para 3.9, although, for the reasons set out there, it is seldom to be recommended to most unsecured and non-preferential creditors.

Table 3.1: Enforcement methods – advantages and disadvantages

Method	Advantages	Disadvantages
County court judgments	• mere threat may provoke payment • may prevent further debts in the future	• can form basis of administration order • having a CCJ is no guarantee of payment • expense
Warrants of execution	• quick • relatively cheap • 'part warrants' can be issued to recover portions of the debt • most effective against business debtors	• may be no goods of value or may be exempt/3rd party property • can be suspended • bailiff may fail to gain entry
Attachments of earnings	• payment guaranteed if wages are paid • regular payments • simple to operate • threat of AEO may lead to payment of CCJ in full • can enforce compliance by committal	• debtor may be low paid • debtor may be dismissed because of AEO • debtor may be self-employed • debtor may lose job • other AEOs may already exist and have priority • other AEOs may be consolidated • an administration order may be made
Third party debt orders	• guaranteed payment if funds exist • may produce lump sum	• may be no funds in the account • account may have been closed • may be hard to get details of bank accounts • may cause future payment problems if the full debt is not cleared
Charging orders	• provides security for debt • can enforce by order for sale • may provoke discharge of CCJ	• may be little or no equity in property • may be a long time before security can be realised • court may refuse order for sale
Examination of means	• gets an overall picture of debtor's circumstances • relatively cheap • can enforce by committal	• produces no money directly • defendant may try to ignore application or may lie to court • may lead to an administration order being made

3.6 Limitations on enforcement

Although Limitation Act 1980, s 24(1) states that an action may only be brought on a judgment within a period of 6 years from the date on which it becomes enforceable, this does not apply to the processes of enforcement of the judgment through the court being described here – although it does apply to bankruptcy and winding up petitions.

There are special limitation rules applicable to the issue of execution (see Chapter 4) and to orders for sale (see Chapter 7), but otherwise there is no restriction upon when enforcement proceedings may be begun. Nevertheless, the judgment debtor could legitimately raise the issue of undue delay before the court and the creditor should be able to give good reasons if a considerable time has passed since default upon the original judgment.

3.7 Information gathering

The necessary implication of para 3.5 is that it will be necessary when choosing any particular form of execution, to gather the necessary information about the debtor's circumstances. There are a number of means by which this may be done:

- conducting a search against an individual's name using one of the credit reference agencies (see addresses in Appendix 2);
- conducting a search of the register held by Registry Trust (see Appendix 2). This provides information not only on judgments of county courts and the High Court, but also administration orders, Child Support Agency liability orders, fines and tribunal awards. Searches cost between £8 and £30 and can clearly be a valuable aid to enforcement, as they will reveal both the extent of an individual's indebtedness and, more crucially, the other competing forms of enforcement currently being pursued against him/her;
- a tracing agency may be used. Fees will be payable for tracing a debtor – between £50 and £100 may be typical for each case. If time has elapsed since the judgment or if the debtor appears to be deliberately avoiding the creditor, this may be a worthwhile expense;
- conducting a search for information upon a company and its officers through Companies House or using a commercial agency;
- client's own records; or,
- application to the court under CPR, Part 71 (see below).

As mentioned in para 3.4, the county court offers the ability to ascertain more personal information about the judgment debtor by means of an examination on oath. This used to be termed an 'oral examination' and the term is still a useful description of the process.

Examinations tend to be used by many creditors as a last resort when other forms of enforcement have failed. The major weakness of the procedure is, of course, that it does depend upon the debtor telling the truth about his/her circumstances when placed on oath. Creditors may also be discouraged from using the process by the duty to pay travel expenses which may arise, by the other costs which will be incurred and by the fact that it might precipitate an administration order. Conversely, an application for an examination is relatively inexpensive, it may gather valuable information which enables another form of enforcement to be used, it may demonstrate to the defendant that the creditor is serious about recovery of the debt and it may simply enable the claimant to re-establish communication with the debtor. Even if the only result is that it reveals to person to be too poor to pay the judgment debt, it may have paid for itself in the expense of time, trouble and fees saved thereby.

3.7.1 Application for examination of means

Under CPR, Part 71 a county court has the power to order a judgment debtor to attend court to provide information about his/her means or about 'any other matter about which information is needed to enforce a judgment or order'.

Application for an examination is made to the court which issued the judgment (unless the case has been transferred) by completing form N316 (for an individual) or N316A (for a limited company) along with confirmation of the balance remaining on the judgment. If an officer of a company is to be examined, the judgment creditor should specify the name and address of the person whom the court should examine. The court's powers under CPR, Part 71 do not extend beyond these individuals – for example, the trustee of a discretionary trust of which the judgment debtor is beneficiary may not be ordered to attend to provide information (see *Franses v Somer al Assad* [2007] EWHC 2442 (Ch)).

The creditor may ask for the examination to be conducted by a judge, but it will be necessary to give reasons for this. Equally, the creditor may ask that when s/he attends court, the debtor is required to answer particular questions or produce specific documents in addition to those normally demanded by the court. The notes to the N316 outline what questions the debtor will be expected to answer and what evidence s/he will have to provide. A fee of £50 is payable at the time of filing the application.

Provided the application is correctly completed, a court officer will take the necessary steps to arrange an examination. The application form will be endorsed as a receipt for the creditor along with the date, time and place fixed for the examination. If the applicant has asked for the questioning to be conducted before a judge, the matter will be referred to a judge for consideration. This will only be allowed where the creditor has set out 'compelling reasons' for the judge to be involved. These might involve the complexity of the defendant's financial affairs or a history of evasion and providing false information on the part of the judgment debtor.

Notice of the application will have to be served personally upon the debtor by either the claimant or by a court officer. With permission of court, another form of service may be permitted – for example, upon the debtor's solicitors (see *Islamic Investment Company of the Gulf (Bahamas) Ltd v Symphony Gems* [2009] EWHC 2378 (Comm)). Notice is given to the defendant on form N39 and allows not less than 14 days' warning of an examination to be held at the court for the district within which s/he resides or does business. The creditor can undertake to arrange service but will have to file an affidavit on form EX550 confirming the following details:

- the manner and date of service;
- whether travel expenses have been requested;
- whether any payments have been received from the debtor; and
- that there is still a balance outstanding on the judgment debt.

The certificate must be sworn into the court no more than 7 days and no less than 2 days before the scheduled date. If the claimant wishes the court to serve the notice, a fee of £100 will be payable. Even if the county court bailiff or HCEO serves the notice, the judgment creditor must still file the affidavit confirming the manner and date of service and the balance outstanding on the judgment debt. If service fails, it will be necessary for the claimant to notify the court so that a new interview date can be arranged. Personal service will then have to be attempted once again.

The debtor is required to attend court to answer questions on oath and to produce any documents which the order may specify. If the defendant is a company, an officer may be summonsed to attend to give evidence on form N38. This may be quite an effective way of provoking a response as a director may often be unhappy about having to attend court to give evidence in such circumstances.

Debtors are entitled, under CPR, r 71.4, to request that the creditor pays his/her reasonable travel expenses to enable them to attend an examination. This request should be made no less than 7 days before the date of the hearing and the creditor must confirm in the affidavit filed in court before the examination whether a claim has been made and has been met or whether the debtor has not asked for expenses. If travel expenses are requested but are not paid, the debtor could not then be committed for a failure to attend the hearing.

3.7.2 Examination

The examination may be conducted either before a court officer or, if the court has ordered it, before a circuit judge. If the hearing is before a court officer, the creditor may attend and ask the additional questions which were specified in the application notice. If the examination is before the judge, the creditor must attend and will be required to conduct the questioning of the debtor. Note that it is possible for the examination to be conducted by video link where the judgment debtor is out of the jurisdiction at the time of the hearing (see *Marketmaker Technology Ltd v CMC Group plc* [2008] EWHC 1556 (QB)).

Examinations are normally conducted by a member of court staff, who completes a standard questionnaire regarding the debtor's income, property, savings and expenses. The prescribed forms for examining individuals or companies are contained in appendices to the practice directions to CPR, Part 71. The debtor is provided with the standard questionnaire to complete on the day (although some courts may send this in advance and may only order to person to attend if they fail to reply or if the judgment creditor is unhappy with the answers that were given). Once the statement has been completed and once the court officer has received answers to any of the additional questions provided by the judgment creditor, the record is checked over by the court officer and questions are asked about any omissions or uncertain answers. The person may be invited to make an offer of payment, the form is signed and sworn and the examination is complete. If the person refuses to sign the questionnaire, this is noted on the record of evidence taken.

If the hearing has been arranged before a judge at the creditor's request, the creditor or his/her representative will conduct the questioning. The standard questionnaires are not employed on such occasions. The hearing will be tape recorded.

Some debtors are very honest and make a full disclosure of their means and assets at the hearing. Many are evasive and will provide only partial information unless they are closely and carefully examined. Some creditors (as a review of the case law will disclose) will endeavour to hinder and avoid the request for information by all available means. The court has powers to deal with such cases, but it can lead to an order to obtain information being a very protracted and frustrating procedure.

3.7.3 Adjournment and non-attendance

If the debtor fails to attend (or fails to bring some of the specified documents) another date for the examination will normally be set. The court will give directions for service of the notice of the new date upon the debtor. The debtor may be allowed another couple of chances to attend before a court officer before this 'final' stage is reached. In one case, after many adjournments due to the ill-health of the defendant and his absence from the country, the court ordered that he provide written answers to the questions rather than adjourn the examination again (see *Islamic Investment Company of the Gulf (Bahamas) Ltd v Symphony Gems* [2009] EWHC 2378 (Comm)).

In some cases if the debtor fails to attend, or if s/he refuses to answer questions or to be placed upon oath, the matter will be referred to a district or circuit judge, who may make a committal order. This should not be done where the creditor has failed to provide travel expenses or has failed to provide the affidavit of service to the court. On the other hand, if the court is satisfied that the N39 notice was properly served, a committal order will be made. Generally, though, this order will be suspended to enable to individual to attend court and provide the information required. Once more it will be necessary for the order to be served personally upon the debtor by either the claimant or the bailiff, following which the affidavit on form EX550 will have to be sworn at court.

3.7.4 Suspended orders

After a suspended committal order has been issued on form N79A, a further examination will take place at the court. If the debtor failed to attend a previous hearing before a judge, or if the terms of the suspended committal order direct this, then the second hearing will be before a judge. Otherwise, a court officer will again conduct the examination.

If the debtor still fails to attend or otherwise refuses to comply, for example by refusing to answer questions or by refusing to be put on oath, a warrant of arrest may be issued to bring the debtor before the court. The arrest warrant is issued on form N40A and the debtor will be brought before either a High Court master or a DJ. Even though the individual may offer to make full payment at this stage, the arrest will still take place. Although very rare, the debtor could still at this stage apply to suspend the committal warrant on form N245. In completing the standard application for suspension, defendants will be supplying a good deal of the information required from them during an examination of means. Alternatively, s/he can simply provide the information which the court requires and this will generally be sufficient. The practice direction to CPR, Part 71 advises that at the hearing a judge should discharge a committal order unless satisfied beyond reasonable doubt that the debtor has failed to comply not only with the original order to attend but also with the subsequent suspended committal order and that both of these were properly served upon him/her.

If the arrested debtor still refuses at this stage to answer the questions or otherwise cooperate, the suspension of the committal warrant is terminated and a committal warrant is issued by the judge on form N40B. This instructs the bailiff or other officer to take the debtor to prison. If the debtor were to be committed, this is of course a punishment for contempt and it will still be necessary for him/her to provide the evidence of means to the court when released.

If, once this information has been supplied, the judge feels that there is sufficient information to make an administration order (see para 3.2) this will be done. The debtor's responses to the examination are then treated as if s/he had completed the application form N92.

3.8 Enforcing a judgment abroad

A judgment creditor may discover that the debtor has moved out of England and Wales or has assets out of the jurisdiction, so that enforcement of a judgment must be conducted in a foreign court.

Detailed provisions exist for the conduct of such cases. The starting point is CPR, Part 74, but there is considerable additional legislation to consider. Only an outline of the procedure is provided here in order to raise some of the key issues relating to this situation. A judgment debtor is very likely to need specialist legal help within the jurisdiction to which s/he wishes to transfer the case. This will add considerably to the expense of recovery action, in addition to the costs of the process of transfer itself.

3.8.1 Enforcement elsewhere in the United Kingdom

If the judgment debtor is resident in either Scotland or Northern Ireland, the process of enforcement against him/her is relatively straightforward. Under CPR, r 74.17 the starting point is for the claimant to apply for a certificate of judgment under Civil Jurisdiction and Judgments Act 1982, s 18 and Sch 6. Application is made to the court in which judgment was entered. The request is made on form N244 giving the following information:

- the details of the parties to the claim;
- the sums payable and still remaining unpaid under the judgment;
- whether interest was allowed by the judgment and, if so, the rate thereof and the amount accrued to the date of the application; and
- lastly, whether the judgment is subject to any appeal or stay.

The relevant court cannot issue the certificate if the relevant appeal period has not expired, if an appeal is pending or if the enforcement of the judgment has been stayed or suspended. Provided these provisos do not apply, the court will issue a certificate which states the amount due under the judgment, including costs and interest, and which confirms that no appeal or stay is in effect.

The judgment creditor then has 6 months within which to register at a court in any other part of the United Kingdom. Registration makes the judgment enforceable as if it were a judgment of the court to which it has been transferred. The reasonable costs and expenses of the registration process may be added and interest may accrue as it would on a judgment of the registering court.

In Northern Ireland the judgment must be registered with the Front of House Office at the Royal Courts of Justice, Chichester Street, Belfast, BT1 3JF. The case will then be passed to the Enforcement of Judgments Office through which attempts at recovery may be made by means of attachment of earnings, seizure of goods, the appointment of a receiver, attachment of debts or an order charging land.

In Scotland, the certificate of judgment is sent to Registers of Scotland, for which a fee of £10 is payable. The judgment will then be treated as equivalent to a decree issued by a sheriff's court and will be enforceable by attachment of earnings, bank account or goods.

3.8.2 Enforcement outside the United Kingdom

If the judgment debtor is resident outside the United Kingdom, very different and far more complex provisions apply. These are further compounded by the language problems which do not exist in cases of enforcement within the United Kingdom – although the differences in terminology and procedure should not be underestimated. Two different procedures exist for recovery, depending on the nature of the debt and the court claim.

52 *Enforcement Preliminaries*

European Enforcement Order

The European Union in 2004 created a simplified procedure for the recovery of certain debts within Europe. This is termed the European Enforcement Order (EEO) (see Appendix to CPR, Part 74, PD 74B or, for full text, Council Regulation (EC) No 805/2004). Special conditions must be satisfied for this streamlined procedure to be applicable:

- the case needs to have been uncontested. This means that the debtor either admitted the claim, never objected to it or, if a defence was filed, s/he never followed it through;
- the debt must not have been incurred for either trade or for professional purposes; and
- the debtor must be a consumer.

If the EEO is available, application is made to the relevant court on form N219 (High Court) or form N219A to a county court for a certificate of judgment. Once issued by the court under CPR, r 74.28, the appropriate court in the relevant country must be sent a copy of the judgment, a copy of the EEO certificate and a translation of the certificate if necessary.

Other cases where EEO does not apply

If the EEO procedure is not available, the judgment creditor will have to rely upon the older process for transferring judgments to other jurisdictions for recovery.

The starting point is to apply to the High Court or a county court for a certified copy of the judgment under CPR, r 74.13. Application is made without notice on form N244. The request must be supported by written evidence on various matters. The applicant must provide a copy of the original claim form and statements of case, along with evidence of their service upon the defendant. The creditor must produce a statement giving the grounds for the judgment and confirmation that the judgment has been properly served upon the defendant. The court must of course know the amount still payable under the judgment and the details of interest allowed under the judgment (the amount accrued to date and the rate of interest payable). Finally, confirmation is required that there is neither an appeal pending nor a stay of execution in place upon the judgment.

Once obtained, the certificate can be filed in the appropriate court of the country to which it is forwarded. These are specified in Brussels Convention on Jurisdiction and the Enforcement of Judgments in Civil and Commercial Matters 1968, Art 32. Article 33 requires the applicant to provide the court with an address for service within the country or the address of lawyer handling the case within that jurisdiction.

3.9 Insolvency

Insolvency procedures are relevant to judgment creditors in two ways. Firstly, they may be considered as a final option for the recovery of a debt. Alternatively, the insolvency of the judgment debtor will have a significant impact upon the ability of the creditor to recover the judgment debt.

3.9.1 Insolvency as a means of debt recovery

A creditor is entitled to issue a bankruptcy petition against an individual debtor where the amount outstanding is at least £750. The courts will always prefer that a petition should be founded upon a prior judgment so that any disputes about liability and the amount due have already been resolved before the courts. That said, it is proper to observe that bankruptcy is not, in reality, a means of enforcing a single debt. Once a bankruptcy order has been made, all the debts owed by the debtor on that date will have to be taken into consideration by the Official Receiver in the administration of the case. It could well transpire that the judgment debt upon which the petition was based is the smallest liability of the debtor. The debts are paid pro-rata from the estate after the (substantial) expenses of the insolvency have been met and after preferential debts (mortgages and certain taxes) have been paid. If there are no assets, the debts will be written off after 12 months.

For all these reasons, bankruptcy is seldom sensibly to be recommended as a means of debt recovery except perhaps in cases where the debtor has indulged in fraudulent business practices or borrowing. Often the main asset in bankruptcy is the debtor's home; a judgment creditor would be far better off pursuing this by means of a charging order than by petitioning for bankruptcy.

In brief, the procedure for bankrupting an individual is as follows:

- *Issue of a statutory demand*: this is a final demand for payment in prescribed form. There is no fee for the issue of the demand and no form of service is prescribed, although personal service is advisable if it is intended that a bankruptcy petition will follow. The demand is in prescribed form (form 6.1 for a liquidated debt or form 6.2 for a debt founded upon a judgment) and gives the debtor 18 days to settle the debt or 21 days to make application to the relevant court with bankruptcy jurisdiction to set the demand aside. This may be done on such grounds as it is secured or there is a counterclaim equalling or exceeding the amount claimed to be due.

Statutory demands should not be issued without the serious intention of following the matter through with a bankruptcy petition. It must be acknowledged that certain creditors and their collection agents do use statutory demands as little more than another 'red letter' in an attempt to put extra pressure upon a debtor. This may be regarded as an abuse of process and is certainly not regarded as good practice by the Office of Fair Trading.

- *Issue of a bankruptcy petition in* the local court with bankruptcy jurisdiction: two forms of petition may be used, form 6.7 where the ground is that the debtor has failed to comply with a statutory demand or form 6.9 where the grounds for seeking insolvency are that execution upon a judgment has been returned wholly or partially unsatisfied. If bailiffs have made serious attempts to levy and have found insufficient to cover the debt, then the creditor will have the basis for a petition. A mere visit by the HCEO will not be sufficient to justify a petition on this ground. In contrast, however, the court will not place a technical meaning on the reference to a 'return' by the bailiff or sheriff. If the facts of the case support the petitioner's claim, for example, the few assets found have been sold for nominal sums, this will be sufficient without the need for a formal return to the writ or warrant (see also Chapter 4) (see *Re A Debtor (No 340 of 1992) ex parte Debtor v First National Commercial Bank plc* [1996] 2 All ER 211, CA; *Skarzynski v Chalford Property Co Ltd* [2001] BPIR 673).

  The cost of the petition is in itself substantial, being currently £190. The above advice against the use of a statutory demand as a mere red letter is reinforced by the fact that the Insolvency Rules 1986 (SI 1986/1925) expect that a petition will normally be filed within 4 months of the expiry of the statutory demand. If the creditor waits longer than this, it will be necessary to give the court an explanation for the delay (CPR, r 6.12(7)).

Similar considerations and procedures apply to petitions to wind-up a limited company. A statutory demand must first be served under Insolvency Act 1986, s 123(1). Unlike in personal insolvencies, however, the demand on form 4.1 merely gives the company 21 days in which to pay a debt of at least £750; there is no option to apply to the court to set it aside. If the debt is not paid, a winding up petition may follow on form 4.2. The fee is again £190.

Debts of partnerships may be pursued by bankruptcy against the partners or by winding up of the partnership (or both).

Table 3.2: Insolvency – advantages and disadvantages

Advantages	Disadvantages
Cost – relatively inexpensive for the recovery of larger debts, especially if only a statutory demand is required	Cost – both in terms of the court fee and the expenses of the trustee and Official Receiver
May be effective against home owners and limited companies	May be few assets of value and certainly of little use against tenants or the unemployed
Serious threat may provoke a response, very possibly at the statutory demand stage	Involves all creditors and the petitioning creditor may be the smallest debt or there may be many preferential or secured creditors
Fairly quick and simple	No good for debts of less than £750
May produce a lump sum payment instead of instalments	Will probably lead to all or part of the debt due being written off

3.9.2 The impact of insolvency on debt recovery

Proper information gathering in advance of any litigation should reveal whether or not the debtor is already insolvent. In any case, the creditor threatening or initiating court action is highly likely to be informed if there is some impediment to that action progressing. Insolvency is therefore most likely to intervene after judgment has already been entered.

The impact of the insolvency will depend upon the form of insolvency involved, when the debt was incurred in relation to the start of the insolvency and the identity of the debtor – whether the defendant is a company or an individual. Each of the main forms of insolvency will be described in turn.

3.9.3 Individual voluntary arrangements

The individual voluntary arrangement (IVA) enables those in debt or facing insolvency to agree with their creditors proposals for the reorganisation of their finances in order to be able to avoid bankruptcy. Creditors are offered a scheme of repayment that should leave them better off than if the person went bankrupt, and the debtor avoids all the stigma and restrictions of actually being an undischarged bankrupt. Enforcement can be effected at two stages in the process of making an IVA:

- *interim orders*: the initial stage of the procedure is for the debtor to formulate repayment proposals with an insolvency practitioner who acts as 'nominee' and draws up a detailed scheme for presentation to the creditors. To buy time for this work to be done, the debtor can apply to the court for an interim order which lasts for 14 days and allows the nominee time to prepare a report for the court on the IVA proposal. Insolvency Act 1986, s 252(2) makes it clear that the effect of the interim order is to establish a moratorium during which no execution or other legal process may be commenced or continued, except with permission of court. Under s 254 whilst an interim order application is pending the court may stay any action, execution or other legal process and may also forbid the levying of any distress on the debtor's property, or its subsequent sale, or both. This provides comprehensive protection against enforcement for the debtor;

- *IVA*: all creditors get a chance to vote upon the scheme at a meeting arranged by the nominee. If 75% by value accept the scheme it comes into effect and all unsecured creditors are bound by it. They must accept the repayments and cannot enforce their debts whilst the IVA remains in force.

3.9.4 Bankruptcy

A bankruptcy order will be made against a debtor on his/her application if the court is satisfied that a debt is due and that the debtor is unable to pay it. The making of the order has a number of effects on the person's finances and property, largely taking away the person's control of their affairs and placing their administration in the hands of a trustee. In return, debtors are given substantial protection from enforcement by their creditors, but it is important to note that this only applies to those creditors whose debts are 'provable' in the bankruptcy. Debts due on the date on which the order was made are 'provable' and will be administered under the bankruptcy. Wholly new debts arising subsequently are not affected by the bankruptcy order and can be enforced in the normal manner:

- *pending petitions*: whilst a petition is pending the bankruptcy court has powers under Insolvency Act 1986, s 285(1) to stay any 'action, execution or other legal process' against the property or person of the debtor (s 285(1)). Equally, the court where the case is taking place may stay proceedings or allow them to continue on terms (s 285(2));

- *effect of bankruptcy order*: enforcement after a bankruptcy order is made is controlled primarily by s 285(3) of the Act. No creditor whose debt is provable in the bankruptcy may take any steps against the person or property of the bankrupt to enforce that debt. Property includes goods, chattels and money (s 436). The effect of this is to completely bar enforcement of an existing debt that is included in the bankruptcy. These restrictions on enforcement are however subject to special rules applying to execution (see below).

If new debts arise the situation is more complex. If there are no existing debts proved for in the bankruptcy then the creditor can proceed with recovery action as normal save that enforcement could be stayed on application under either Insolvency Act 1986, s 285(1) or s 285(2). In most cases there may be little reason for the court to bar enforcement as bankruptcy does not absolve the debtor of responsibility for ongoing or subsequent liabilities. However, if the creditor has already proved for a debt in the bankruptcy, permission of court is required at any time before the person is discharged in order to pursue any debt arising after the order under s 285(3)(b) of the Act.

Special provisions are made in respect of the conduct of levies of execution by an HCEO and county court bailiff. Basically, if the execution has not been completed by sale of the seized goods, the creditor will not be entitled to retain the benefit of the execution. 'Completion' of an execution will require the process to have reached a stage such as sale of the goods, receipt of the proceeds of sale by the judgment creditor or full payment of the sum being enforced before the bankruptcy petition was presented. Conversely, an execution is not complete where (for instance) instalments have been agreed, the bailiff has withdrawn upon the instructions of the execution creditor, the bailiff has merely taken possession of goods or has removed without yet having conducted a sale or a sale has taken place but the proceeds are still in the hands of the county court bailiff or HCEO. This is however a complex area and the creditor's rights may depend upon the exact stage reached by the bailiff and the conduct of the creditor and debtor (see John Kruse, *Law of Seizure of Goods* (Hammicks, 2nd edn, 2009), para 4.3.3).

3.9.5 County court administration order

As described earlier, taking court action against a debtor may enable that person to apply to court for an administration order. If this happens, the enforcement of that debt and others outstanding will be affected.

Under County Courts Act 1984, s 114, just as in bankruptcy, all enforcement against either the property or person of the debtor is barred for debts which are scheduled to (included in) the administration order. However, it is also worth noting that this inhibition also applies to debts which were included in the debtor's application to the court – even though the DJ accepted the creditor's objections and consented to exclude the debt from the order itself. This is unlikely to apply to unsecured, consumer debts, which DJs will tend to include without hesitation. In either case, though, enforcement will only be able to proceed with permission of the court and on such conditions as the court may impose. The creditor will need to apply for permission on form N244.

3.9.6 Debt relief orders

Tribunals, Courts and Enforcement Act 2007 (TCEA 2007), s 103 amends the Insolvency Act 1986 by inserting a new Part 7A. The contents of this new part are set out in TCEA 2007, Sch 17; it creates a new procedure termed debt relief orders.

An individual who is unable to pay his debts of less than £15,000 may apply for a debt relief order. If the person has no assets nor surplus income of more than £50 monthly, the Insolvency Service will make the order.

The order imposes a moratorium upon the recovery of the debts included in it. The effect of this is that, whilst it lasts, the creditor has no remedy in respect of the debt, and may not commence any action or other legal proceedings against the debtor for the debt, except with the permission of the court and on such terms as the court may impose. If, on the date on which the order comes into effect, a creditor has any petition, action or other proceeding pending in any court, the court may stay those proceedings or allow them to continue on such terms as the court thinks fit.

The moratorium relating to the qualifying debts specified in a debt relief order continues for the period of one year beginning with the date for the order, unless the moratorium terminates early or the moratorium period is extended by the official receiver or by the court. At the end of the year, as in bankruptcy, the debts will be discharged. New debts arising after the making of the debt relief order will not be part of it and will not be affected by the moratorium on recovery.

3.9.7 Company administration orders

The rules on company administration orders and upon administrators in insolvency generally were altered by the Enterprise Act 2002. This inserted into the Insolvency Act 1986 a new Sch B1, which replaced the previous Part II of the 1986 Act dealing with administration orders.

A company in financial difficulty may protect itself from its creditors and create a breathing space in which it may restructure by applying to the court for an administration order (Sch B1, para 12):

- *pending applications*: under para 44, when an application is presented, and until the order is made or dismissed, an interim moratorium is in effect. A moratorium also applies for 14 days when a notice of an intention to appoint an administrator is filed in court. The terms of the moratorium are as described below under para 43;
- *administration orders*: if an order is made, an administrator (an insolvency practitioner) is appointed and must notify all creditors that, for the period that the order is in force, s/he will be managing the company's business and property. To facilitate this process the firm is comprehensively protected from enforcement (para 43). No legal process may be instituted or continued against the company except with either the consent of the administrator or the permission of the court. Legal process is defined as including legal proceedings and execution. If the court does give permission to proceed, it may impose conditions.

3.9.8 Compulsory winding up

A creditor may apply to court for a company to be declared insolvent and be liquidated or 'wound up'. It is also possible for the firm to petition itself in order to gain the protection of the court. A winding up petition may be presented if one of a number of grounds is satisfied but the most common is that the company is unable to pay its debts. If a winding up order is made, all creditors are affected; no distinction is made between pre or post-insolvency 'provable' debts as in personal bankruptcy:

- *enforcement after petition*: under Insolvency Act 1986, s 126(1), between the presentation of the petition and an order being made, any action or proceeding pending against the company in either the High Court or Court of Appeal can be stayed. In addition, any other pending action or proceeding may be restrained by the bankruptcy court. Clearly this will affect court actions for debt recovery and enforcement;
- *enforcement after the winding up order*: Insolvency Act 1986, ss 128 and 130 deal with the protection afforded a company during winding up by the court. Under s 128 any proceedings or execution are void if initiated after the winding up commenced, ie after the petition was presented. All debts are effected. There is no differentiation between that for pre-insolvency provable debts and post-insolvency non-provable debts unlike bankruptcy.

This apparent bar on enforcement is, however, subject to the powers contained in Insolvency Act 1986, s 130(2). Under this provision no action or proceeding can be begun or continued *after* an order has been made, *except* with the permission of the insolvency court and on such terms as the court may impose. Where the enforcement began before the commencement of the winding up, and unless special reasons exist which render it inequitable, such as fraud or unfair dealing, it will generally be allowed to continue. Permission to proceed may therefore be given where, for example, the debtor has deliberately delayed enforcement of the debt or where there are ample assets available for all creditors of the insolvent company. The court will normally refuse to allow an execution to continue where this would mean involve injury to, or the unfair treatment of, other creditors in the insolvency. Conversely, where the enforcement was begun after the winding up commenced, it will only be allowed where special circumstances apply. These might include the delay or obstruction of the creditor by the debtor company. There is considerable case law authority on the interpretation of these provisions (see John Kruse, *Law of Seizure of Goods* (Hammicks, 2nd edn, 2009) for detailed discussion of the case law).

These same provisions apply to voluntary liquidations and to partnership insolvencies.

3.10 Stays of execution

The court has a general discretion to impose a stay upon the execution of a judgment. This power will be exercised having taken into account all the circumstances of the case and having weighed up the respective interest of judgment creditor and debtor.

3.10.1 High Court powers

The court can stay execution if it is satisfied that the conditions set out in CPR, Sch 1: RSC, Ord 47, r 1 are met and either there are *'special circumstances which render it inexpedient to enforce the judgment or order'* or *'the applicant is unable from any cause to pay money'*. The court will require the defendant to attend to be examined on the evidence given provided in the application for the stay and to produce supporting documentation such as witness statements providing details of current outgoings, sources of income and other liabilities, especially if there is any doubt about the individual's probity (see *Gulf Azov Shipping Co Ltd v Egbe* [2003] EWCA Civ 1823).

This discretion to permit a stay upon recovery must be exercised in light of the fact that the court should normally give most weight to creditors' rights to enforce their judgments. Parliament has granted the choice of when and how to enforce a judgment to the judgment creditor, not to the court, so the court should only interfere with a judgment creditor's rights where there is 'good reason' because of the 'exceptional circumstances' of the debtor. The court should certainly not exercise its discretion to interfere where no substantial payment can be made as it must also have regard to the hardship which non-payment of the judgment might cause. Even when a stay is granted, it may only be for a limited period of time, perhaps pending the outcome of other proceedings or because the court is satisfied that there is a realistic prospect of the debt being cleared by substantial instalment payments over a matter of weeks or months (see CPR, Sch 2: RSC, Ord 45, r 11 and Ord 47, r 1; *Amsalem t/a MRE Building Contractors v Raivid & Raivid* [2009] EWHC 3226 (TCC); *Jacques & Another (trading as C & E Jacques Partnership v Ensign Contractors Ltd* [2009] EWHC 3383 (TCC); *Winchester Cigarette Machinery Ltd v Payne (No 2)* (1993) *The Times*, 15 December; *General Mutual Life Assurance Society v Feltwell Fen 2nd District Drainage Board* [1945] KB 394).

The court has broad discretion to stay the execution either absolutely or for such period and subject to such conditions as it thinks fit. Accordingly, orders staying execution that the court may make include the following:

- a stay on terms of payment of the debt, whether by instalments or by a lump sum or sums;

- a stay of terms of payment of security into court (see *Continental Tranfert Technique Ltd v Federal Government of Nigeria*, QBD (Comm), 31 March 2010, unreported – execution be stayed on payment of £100 million security within a set time);

- an indefinite stay with liberty to apply or for a set period with a review at the end thereof;

- a stay on recovery of only part of the judgment debt;

- a stay subject to a moratorium for a set period; or

- a stay subject to a charging order (if the debtor consents).

Readers should also note that under CPR, Sch 1: RSC, Ord 45, r 11 the court has a general power to stay execution of a judgment or order, and to give other relief, on the ground of matters that have arisen since the date upon which the judgment was entered. A stay may be ordered on whatever terms the court thinks just. It has been held that the effect of this provision is to enable the court to consider matters which would have prevented the original order being made, or which would have led to a stay if they had already arisen at the date of the order (see *London Permanent Building Society v De Baer* [1969] 1 Ch 321).

Arguments under European Convention on Human Rights, Art 8 and First Protocol, Art 1 have been advanced in favour of courts granting stays. These have largely met with an unfavourable reaction from judges. The jurisprudence of the Strasbourg Court also requires wider factors to be considered than just the circumstances of the debtor. Refusing a stay of execution has been said to be 'necessary in a democratic society' for the protection of contractual rights (see *Society of Lloyds v Surman* [2004] EWHC 2967 (Ch)).

Execution may also be stayed where a judgment is being appealed. This by application under CPR, r 52.7 and special circumstances will have to be firmly established in order to persuade the court of the need to deprive claimants of their rights. Even if such special grounds are demonstrated, the court will still wish to take heed of all the circumstances surrounding the case up until that point, the conduct of the parties (in particular that of the defendant seeking the stay) and, especially, the risk of irremediable harm or injustice to one party or another by refusing a stay (see *Defra v Downs* [2009] EWCA Civ 257; *Gater Assets v Nak Naftogaz Ukrainiy* [2008] EWCA Civ 1051). The special circumstances which may persuade the court to permit a stay include the possibility of enforcement ruining or precipitating the bankruptcy of the defendant or the likelihood that if the debt or damages were to be paid to the claimant, they would not be recoverable if the appeal were successful. If such an issue is a concern, payment into court may be required (see *Barker v Lavery* [1885] 14 QBD 709; *GE Capital Bank v Rushton* [2005] EWCA Civ 1393; *Dumford Trading AG v OAO Atlantrybflot* [2004] EWCA Civ 1265; *RBS v Fielding* [2003] EWCA Civ 988; *Nicholl v Rye* [1999] EWHC 710 (Admin)). The mere existence of an arguable ground for an appeal is not, by itself, a good reason for imposing a stay. Stays may be on terms such as a requirement that the claimant be paid without undue delay if the appeal fails, that a sum is paid into court by the defendant or that the appellant's assets are preserved in the meantime, other than for satisfying essential liabilities (see *Linotype-Hell Finance Ltd v Baker* [1993] 1 WLR 321; *Simonite v Sheffield City Council* (1992) *The Times*, 29 December 1992; *The Annot Lyle* [1886] 11 P 114).

Finally, execution may be stayed where the continued enforcement of the judgment would conflict with the terms of an order made in insolvency proceedings (see para 3.9.1) (see *El Ajou v Stern* [2006] EWHC 3067 (Ch) – an IVA had been agreed).

3.10.2 County court powers

Under County Courts Act 1984, s 88, a county court has a general power to stay any execution issued in proceedings, whether for the whole sum due or an instalment thereon, where the paying party is unable for any reason to satisfy the order. This stay may be on such terms and for such periods as the court thinks fit, and may be renewed periodically until the cause of the inability to pay has ceased. The court also has powers under s 71(2) of the Act to suspend or stay any judgment or order where the person cannot pay the whole sum or any instalment. This can be done for such time and on such terms as the court thinks fit, and can be renewed periodically. This provision is slightly broader in its application than s 88 and the powers found in CPR, Sch 2: CCR, Ord 25 to suspend execution on a judgment and can be of particular help where the defendant cannot pay at all. As in the High Court, execution may be stayed on application where a judgment is being appealed either to a Circuit Judge (CPR, r 52.7) or to the Court of Appeal (s 77).

3.10.3 Stays of execution in practice

Readers will most commonly encounter applications for stays upon enforcement at certain specific points in the recovery process:

- *at the time of judgment*, if a request for payment by instalments is made by the defendant (see para 2.3.2);

- *after default in payment*, the defendant may request that an instalment order is made or that its terms are varied (see para 2.3.2);

- *in response to the issue of execution against goods*: the judgment debtor may apply to suspend the warrant on terms of instalment payment (see para 4.8);

- *at the time of the making of a final charging order*: the court may choose to impose terms postponing enforcement of the charge so long as payment terms are adhered to by the judgment debtor (see para 7.3); and

- *at the time of making an order for sale*: once again the court may choose to postpone the enforcement of the order on terms (see para 7.5.3).

Table 3.3: Elements of effective enforcement

Remedy	Essential	Desirable/optional
Order to provide information	Court fees Fees for bailiff service or for a process server	Additional questions or documents required from debtor
Warrant of execution	Court fees Address(es) for debtor	Details of assets to which bailiff can be directed Awareness of potential adverse claims
Third party debt order	Court fees Name of third party debtor	Fuller details of the accounts or sums owed to judgment debtor Awareness of possible adverse claims Fees for process server
Charging order	Fees for court and Land Registry Details of property or assets owned by debtor	Details of other creditors or claims to the property to be charged Fees for process server
Attachment of earnings order	Court fees Knowledge that debtor receives attachable earnings	Identity of employer and level of earnings Knowledge of possible competing orders or debts
Receiver by way of equitable execution	Court fees Information as to attachable assets, their value, etc Suitable individual prepared to act as receiver	Fees for process server

4 Execution against Goods

4.1 Introduction

The issue of a warrant of execution for the seizure and sale of goods from the debtor's premises is the commonest form of enforcement of judgments. It should not be supposed, however, that frequency of use necessarily indicates high levels of success or large reductions in the debt as a result; the main motivating factor behind many of the warrants issued to bailiffs is that the creditor does not have to undertake any further research before enforcement may proceed. All the bailiff requires is an address at which to call – and that is already in the creditor's possession as it is a necessary fundamental to taking any action at all.

Seizures of goods in general, and civil court seizures in particular, have their problems. There may be nothing worth seizing at the debtor's premises, in which case the entire fee is wasted. The warrant may be suspended on application by the debtor so that the court allows the person to carry on paying the same, or lower, instalments. Some creditors complain that county court bailiffs are not sufficiently 'aggressive' in their pursuit of the matter, which is why some prefer to try execution through the High Court (see para 4.2).

Although the 'logical' conclusion of the issue of a warrant is the sale of the debtor's goods, sales are in fact extremely rare, forming only a very small percentage of the total warrants issued each year. What is effective in the use of warrants is their threat value. It is the fear of sale of goods (however unlikely that may in reality be) which prompts the debtor to pay.

It will be clear that careful thought should still be given to the decision to issue a warrant of execution. The remedy should be matched to the known circumstances of the debtor. A levy against a business may be a very effective strategy, as there may be valuable assets available which are unencumbered by personal claims or protected as exempt basic goods but which at the same time are essential for the continued trading of the business. Difficulties of entry to premises will arise far less frequently. Levies at domestic premises are far less likely to find large quantities of seizable goods and are far less likely to raise substantial amounts of money and they may accordingly be less worthwhile. (For more detail on seizures of goods, see John Kruse, *Law of Seizure of Goods* (Hammicks, 2nd edn, 2009), and John Kruse, *Powers of distress* (Wildy, Simmonds & Hill, 2009).) Figure 4.1 (see p 83) outlines the process for enforcing a judgment by warrant.

4.2 Transfer to the High Court

In the majority of cases, execution against goods issued on a CCJ will be levied by the county court bailiff. However, the jurisdictional rules relating to county courts and the High Court permit some claimants to transfer a case to the High Court for enforcement and, for the reasons mentioned in the previous section, some creditors prefer to follow this route.

Under High Court and County Court Jurisdiction Order 1991 (SI 1991/0724), art 8, the rules on execution are as follows:

- *judgments over £5000* must be enforced by execution in the High Court;
- *judgments for less than £600* cannot be enforced by execution except in the county court;
- *judgments for between £600 and £5000* may be enforced in whichever court the claimant chooses.

For execution to take place in the High Court, the judgment must be transferred from a county court in accordance with the procedure laid down in CPR, Sch 2: CCR, Ord 22, r 8. Cases may be transferred by two methods:

- *by the claimant*: the claimant completes form N293A – this is a combined request for a certificate of the judgment in a county court and a request for the issue of execution in the High Court (termed a writ of *fieri facias*). The N293A requires details of the judgment, the additional costs incurred since that date, the total of interest which has accrued and the rate being charged. The issue of the certificate by a county court acts as an order transferring the case to the High Court. Upon transfer the case ceases to be a CCJ; the parties are notified of this on form N328. The certificate is then presented at the relevant High Court registry and is allocated a reference number, at which point it becomes a High Court judgment upon which interest starts to accrue at the statutory rate. A fee of £50 will also be payable to the court for sealing the writ of execution. For former CCJs of less than £5000 the interest accrues from the date of transfer; for cases of more than £5000 the interest accrues from the date of judgment. The HCEO is then instructed to levy against the debtor; or

- *by an HCEO*: HCEOs offer a free transfer service to judgment creditors. All that is required is to contact the office of an HCEO. This may be the officer for the area in which the judgment debtor resides or does business or it may be any officer anywhere in England and Wales – in these latter cases the writ is allocated to the next available officer for execution. The contact details of HCEOs can be found through the website of the High Court Enforcement Officers Association (see Appendix 2). All the HCEO will need to see is the CCJ. Again, the £50 fee for sealing the writ is payable.

Note, however, that there are circumstances in which an immediate transfer to the High Court may not be possible. If the request from the judgment creditor is made but the court also has pending certain applications from the judgment debtor, no certificate will be issued until the outstanding matter has been determined. These are:

- a request for variation of the date of payment of the judgment or the rate at which it is paid;
- an application made under CPR, r 39.3(3) to set aside the judgment entered after a trial because the defendant was absent from the hearing. Such an application can only be made by the defendant if s/he acts promptly, there was good reason for the failure to attend and the defence to the claim had a reasonable prospect of being successful;
- application to set aside or to vary the judgment under CPR, r 13.4;
- a request for an administration order; or
- an application for a stay on execution under County Courts Act 1984, s 88.

It is to be assumed that, in most of these cases, a decision favourable to the applicant defendant will lead to refusal to transfer on the part of the court.

HCEOs do not possess powers materially different from those of a county court bailiff. The procedures they follow may differ in detail, but overall the process of execution in each court is identical. The same rules as to exempt and third party goods apply and debtors may make application to suspend execution just as in the county court. Both county court bailiffs and HCEOs have obligations to both parties and see themselves as impartial judicial officers responsible for the protection of the legal rights of debtors as well as creditors.

That being the case, what are the reasons for wanting to transfer a judgment of between £600 and £5000 for execution? Creditors prefer HCEOs primarily because they are perceived as more effective than county court bailiffs. This perception arises from the fact that an HCEO is a private bailiff. S/he may be an officer of the Supreme Court but, unlike the county court bailiff, who is an employee of HM Courts Service, the HCEO is not a civil servant and is an employee of a commercial enterprise. HCEOs are motivated by profit and by differing standards of customer service. This factor may boost their effectiveness, but there is a potential price to pay for this. Some HCEOs charge substantial, if not exorbitant, fees for their services. These are levied from the debtor, but they will reduce the return to the creditor and will add to the burden faced by debtors experiencing genuine financial hardship. The decision over transfer to the High Court may therefore be presented as a moral as well as a commercial and legal question.

If the HCEO fails to enforce the writ a 'return' or report will be made to this effect to the judgment creditor. A fee of £60 plus VAT will be payable for the return of what is termed an 'abortive' writ. Nonetheless, if nothing else has been gained, the judgment creditor may have received a report on the debtor's circumstances which may enable better informed choices about future enforcement to be made.

4.3 Issue of warrants

If payments are behind on a CCJ, a warrant of execution may be issued for the whole amount of the judgment then outstanding or, alternatively, for a smaller amount of not less than £50 or one month's (or 4 weeks') instalments, whichever is the greater. These so-called 'part warrants' are in fact very popular – they give the creditor the option to enforce a relatively small amount which there is perhaps a greater prospect of raising out of chattels (especially domestic chattels) or which may provoke a lump sum payment from the defendant to discharge the warrant and avoid further enforcement proceedings.

Application is made by filing in a county court a request on form N323 certifying the sum due and the arrears on the judgment. A fee is payable – currently £100. The form is endorsed as a receipt by the court office with details of the date of issue and the number of the warrant. Form N42 is passed to the bailiff and serves as the warrant that instructs him. If the debtor is not resident in the court of issue, the warrant will be transferred to the local court and will also be allocated a local reference or 'foreign warrant' number for the duration of the time it is in the hands of that court's bailiff. The issue fee (and any other costs incurred later on sale or on withdrawal or cessation of the warrant) are added to the judgment debt to be cleared by payments received or by the proceeds of sale of the goods.

Two or more 'concurrent' warrants may be issued for execution in different county courts. For example if a company has premises within several county court districts, concurrent warrants may be issued, but no more than the total judgment debt may be collected under all the warrants. The costs of only one warrant may be added onto the judgment debt unless permission of court is obtained to allow more to be recovered (CPR, Sch 2: CCR, Ord 26, r 4).

4.4 Issue and limitations

Where 6 years or more have elapsed since the date of entry of the judgment, it is necessary for the judgment creditor to obtain leave of court before issuing execution. Application is made without notice on form N244 supported by an affidavit, though the High Court may direct that the application is made by claim form and a county court may direct that notice be served on the judgment debtor, so that s/he would have an opportunity to make representations (see CPR, Sch 1: RSC, Ord 46, r 2(1)(a); CPR, Sch 2: CCR, Ord 26, r 5(1)(a)).

The guidance from case law is that the court should only allow extra time to the creditor to enforce in exceptional cases and because it is plainly or demonstrably just to do so. The onus of proof lies with the creditor; compelling evidence will be required to take the case out of the ordinary. Accordingly, permission will only be granted where a reasonable explanation of the delay can be provided by the creditor and when the court feels that one of a number of conditions has been satisfied:

- What was the cause of the delay – was it creditor inaction or, perhaps, administrative problems on the part of the court?
- Has the creditor remained active in trying to recover the judgment or has the defendant been given the impression that the matter has been abandoned?
- Has the creditor discovered new assets about which they were previously unaware or which did not exist when execution was tried before?

Prejudice to the debtor will be assumed to arise from any delay in enforcement – and this will increase the longer it is since judgment was entered (see *National Westminster Bank v Powney* [1991] Ch 339; *Duer v Frazer* [2001] 1 All ER 249; *Patel v Singh* [2002] EWCA Civ 1938; *The Society of Lloyds v Longtin* [2005] EWHC 2492 (Comm); *Good Challenger*

Navegante SA v Metalimportexport SA [2003] EWCA Civ 1668). Failure to apply for leave is an abuse of process and the execution may be set aside by the court on application by the debtor. The Limitation Act 1980 does not apply to applications for leave to issue execution as a distinction is made between the right to bring a claim and the procedural right or remedy to issue execution (see *LB Hackney v White* [1995] 28 HLR 219; *National Westminster Bank v Powney* [1990] 2 WLR 1084; *Berliner Industriebank Aktiengesellschaft v Jost* [1971] 1 QB 278; *W T Lamb & Sons v Rider* [1948] 2 KB 331).

Once permission has been obtained, High Court and county court warrants are then valid for 12 months from the date of issue, but they can be extended, or the permission renewed, if necessary. Application for renewal should be made before the 12-month period of validity has expired, but the court can allow the creditor longer. If a warrant is extended, it will be treated as having priority over other warrants that may be issued against the judgment debtor from the original date of its issue. An identical procedure applies to writs of *fieri facias* issued in the High Court (see CPR, Sch 1: RSC, Ord 46, r 2(3); CPR, Sch 2: CCR, Ord 26, r 6).

4.5 Levy process

The process of levy is outlined solely for purposes of information. This stage will be entirely in the hands of the enforcement agent and is something over which the judgment creditor has little control.

4.5.1 Notice to debtor

The defendant normally receives a warning letter on form N326 giving at least 7 days' notice of the warrant's issue and the bailiff's intention to levy (although a DJ may make an order dispensing with notice). If no payment is then made the bailiff will call and endeavour to execute the warrant. It may be thought that notice is counter-productive, as it will give the debtor an opportunity to hide or remove valuable assets. In the vast majority of cases this does not happen as taking such steps is simply too inconvenient or costly for the debtor. The actual effect may be for payment to be made without the necessity for any further steps to be taken.

HCEOs issue a similar notice on form 55 under CPR, Sch 1: RSC, Ord 45, r 2.

4.5.2 Visits and entry

County court bailiffs will typically call two or three times to try to gain entry to the premises. Initial entry cannot be forced to domestic properties but it is possible for bailiffs to force entry to premises such as shops, factories and industrial units (see *Penton v Browne* (1664) 1 Keb 698; *Hodder v Williams* [1895] 2 QB 663). The case law indicates that the bailiff should always enquire as to the presence of seizable goods before forcing entry; in the county court permission of the DJ will be required first and the court may also require an indemnity from the claimant. Where an indemnity is requested, prompt payment will be essential as the court will take no further action on the warrant until it is received (see *Hobson v Thelluson* [1867] 2 QB 642).

4.5.3 Levying on goods

If entry is gained the bailiff will then seek to seize and secure sufficient goods to cover the debt and costs outstanding. There is no reason why the claimant may not, on form N323, direct the bailiff towards certain goods (or premises). There are a number of items which the bailiff may not seize. These are:

- fixtures and fittings;

- goods owned by third parties: this might include property owned solely by the partner or spouse of the debtor, items on hire or hire purchase or subject to various commercial claims. In a levy on business premises goods subject to retention of title clauses, leases, bills of sale, sale or return agreements or similar arrangements may be encountered. Although otherwise attractive, this is the potential risk and expense of levies at factories, workshops and the like. In this context it should also be noted that property already levied by a bailiff for another debt may also not be seized;

- 'such tools, books, vehicles and other items of equipment as are necessary for use personally in business, employment or vocation': attempts to limit this exemption to tools only capable of being carried by the debtor are incorrect; however in the unreported Court of Appeal decision in *Sheriff of Bedford & Toseland Building Supplies Ltd v Bishop* (1993) it was held that if a tool was occasionally used by another, it was not protected. Accordingly, if the debtor is self-employed, a claim may only validly be made if the tools or vehicles in question are only ever used by the debtor. If s/he has employees or employs subcontractors who on occasion may use these items, they will fall outside the exemption (see CCA 1981, s 89(1)(a)(i)); and

- 'such clothing, bedding, furniture, household equipment and provisions as are necessary for satisfying the basic domestic needs of the person and family': it may be difficult for a debtor to argue that such items as personal jewellery or watches should be protected as basic items of clothing. Guidance to the court bailiffs assists in the determination of whether an item is exempt for not – for example, a microwave might be seized if there was a standard oven available and a table and chairs might be taken where some alternative form of seating was left (see CCA 1981, s 89(1)(a)(ii)).

The goods seized will be listed on an inventory and will then be 'impounded'. This process involves placing them in legal custody, thereby giving them legal protection from interference by the debtor or others (it is an offence under CCA 1981, s 92 to interfere with impounded goods) and also entitling the bailiff to later sell the good if necessary. Impounding is usually achieved by taking 'walking possession' of the goods. This involves the goods being left in the premises where they were seized, but subject to a signed agreement made with the debtor or a member of the household which acknowledges their altered status and the bailiff's ongoing rights over them. The walking possession agreement gives the debtor the opportunity to raise the money to prevent sale – or to apply to the court to suspend the warrant subject to instalments (see para 4.8). In levies against business premises, and where the item seized is a motor vehicle, immediate removal by the bailiff to a place of storage is more likely.

4.5.4 Returns and reissues

If the bailiff has not executed the warrant within one month of the date of its issue, he is required by CPR, Sch 2: CCR, Ord 25, r 7(2) to issue a notice to the judgment creditor advising of the delay and providing an explanation for it. This will have to be repeated every successive month thereafter during which the warrant remains unexecuted.

If the bailiff finds that there are no goods worth taking, a 'return' to this effect is made to the court (sometimes referred to as *nulla bona*). Notice of this outcome is served on the judgment creditor on form N317. Other methods of recovery will then have to be considered – one may be a bankruptcy petition founded upon the bailiffs' failure to levy (see para 3.9.1).

If it later comes to the claimant's knowledge that the debtor has acquired assets which would be liable to seizure in execution, it is possible to apply on form N445 for the warrant to be reissued. Where a warrant is reissued, other warrants issued in the interim will be treated as having priority (see *Hunt v Hooper* (1844) 12 M&W 604).

4.6 Levies against partnerships

The goods of partnerships are afforded special treatment in execution. The rule set out in CPR, Part 70, PD 6A.1 is that execution under a judgment against a firm can be levied against any of the following:

- any property owned by the firm;
- the property of any person who admitted to being a partner;
- the property of any person was held by the judgment to be a partner; and
- the property of any person who was served with the claim and who failed to respond to it or to attend hearings.

The fact that the membership of a partnership has changed is no bar to enforcement. Retirement will not prevent execution, nor will death of a partner after issue of the claim (see *Re Frank Hill ex p Holt & Co* [1921] 2 KB 831; *Ellis v Wadeson* [1899] 1 QB 714). Each individual partner can be separately pursued by execution, but a claim against a firm must lead to a judgment against the firm, not just one partner, otherwise a claim for wrongful execution and detention of goods may be made (see *Clark v Cullen* [1882] 9 QBD 355; *Jackson v Litchfield* [1882] 8 QBD 474). Similarly, if judgment is obtained against several named individuals, the warrant must also be issued against them all (see *Penoyer v Bruce* (1697) 1 Ld Raym 244; *Clark v Clement* (1796) 6 TR 525). That said, a warrant does not have to be levied on all or any one or more of those joint judgment debtors (see *Herries v Jamieson* (1794) 5 TR 556). If execution against one partner clears the debt, the others may not of course be pursued. There is no requirement that partnership property be seized before the private property of partners, or vice versa.

Execution may not be issued against a person who was out of the country when the claim form was issued unless:

- s/he was served within England and Wales;
- permission of court was obtained for service of the claim form outside the jurisdiction; or
- (in the High Court only) the person responded to the claim as a partner.

Partners who were out of England and Wales when the action commenced are not otherwise effected.

In addition, permission can be sought under CPR, Part 70, PDs 6A.3 and 6A.4 to issue execution against a person claimed to be a partner. This gives the alleged partner an opportunity to contest the claim of liability and the dispute may be tried as the court directs. Permission cannot be given to issue execution against a person who leaves the firm before an action begins, but the court may allow execution to proceed where a person has 'held themselves out' to be a partner (see *Wigram v Cox* [1894] 1 QB 792; *Davis v Hyman & Co* [1903] 1 KB 854).

Under Partnership Act 1890, s 23(1) the execution made not be made against partnership property for the separate debt of a partner. If this were to happen the partners could interplead (see para 4.9). Note that in *Flude Ltd v Goldberg* [1916] 1 KB 662, a person interpleaded over goods claimed as his sole property. On hearing the case it was decided that the goods were in fact partnership property of the interpleader claimant and the defendant, but as the interpleader claimant had not claimed on this basis the claim to the goods was barred (see *Peake v Carter* [1916] 1 KB 652). In such cases of joint ownership the remedy for the judgment creditor is to apply for a charging order (see para 7.7).

4.7 Sale

If there is neither payment of the judgment debt, nor an offer to discharge the sums due, the bailiff may return after a minimum period of five days and remove the goods for sale (CCA 1981, s 93). At this point entry may be forced. HM Courts Service guidelines require the bailiff to obtain permission from the DJ first and the court may in turn require an indemnity for the costs from the claimant before moving to this stage. This is especially likely to be the case if the bailiff's valuation of the goods indicates that they are insufficient to cover the costs of removal and sale, yet the judgment creditor is insistent upon proceeding. Case law also provides guidance on this matter: entry should only be forced where re-entry is being deliberately refused. It is accordingly obligatory for the bailiff to give prior notice to the debtor of the planned removal. If s/he then chooses to be absent from the premises at the date and time specified, it will be acceptable for a locksmith to be used to gain access (see *Khazanchi v Faircharm Investments* [1998] 2 All ER 901).

A public auction will be arranged and the debtor will receive details in advance, giving another opportunity for full payment to be made. Form N330 is used to notify the creditor either that a sale will take place or that a payment has been received by the court in response to the warrant. In the absence of any payment to discharge the execution, the goods are sold to cover the debt and costs, but no reserve price is set and it is accepted that the return from public auctions, albeit low, represent a 'reasonable price' for the goods. The claimant will receive details of the outcome of the sale on form N444. There is every likelihood that, except in the case of part warrants, a balance will still be outstanding on the judgment at the end of the process. This partly explains why auction sales are so rare.

Although sale by public auction is the normal procedure, an execution creditor is entitled under CCR, Ord 26, r 1(4) to make an application for a private sale to be held. The county court cannot allow private sale if the judgment debt is under £20 (CCA 1981, s 97). If such a request is received, the court will supply to the creditor the details of any other warrants currently outstanding against the judgment debtor. The creditor will then have to serve upon them notice of the application for private sale, giving at least 4 days' notice of the hearing date. Service of notice to the creditors on the list will have to be confirmed to the court at the hearing. The other execution creditors may then attend, along with the judgment debtor, to make representations on the matter. A private sale might be justified where the goods seized are of a specialist nature. Under CPR, Sch 1: RSC, Ord 47, r 6 an identical process applies to writs of *fieri facias* being levied by HCEOs.

4.8 Suspension and withdrawal of warrants and writs

Ongoing execution against goods may be stayed by a debtor by making application to either a county court or the High Court.

4.8.1 Suspension of warrants

It is possible for a debtor to make an application to suspend the warrant under County Courts Act 1984, s 71 and CPR, Sch 2: CCR, Ord 25, r 8. Suspension means that the warrant is stayed so long as the debtor then maintains the payments s/he has proposed and if the terms of suspension of the warrant are not adhered to by the judgment debtor, the creditor may seek reissue of the warrant under CCR, Ord 25, r 8(9). However, in reality it seems that when a suspension is ordered most bailiffs simply make a final return on the warrant to the court and the execution is terminated. Issue of a new warrant on payment of another fee would then be required if execution were to be attempted again by the claimant.

The defendant may apply for suspension on form N245, paying a fee of £35. Details are sent to the claimant on form N246A and three responses are then possible. The judgment creditor may:

- accept the payment proposals made on the form, in which case the court will make an order suspending the warrant on those terms;

76 Execution against Goods

- consent to suspension but not on the terms proposed by the debtor. If the level of instalments are disputed, the matter will be determined by court staff and may be reconsidered by a DJ on application from either party, following the procedure described in para 2.3.2; or

- refuse both the suspension and the offer of payment. In such cases a hearing will be arranged before a DJ at the debtor's local court. The DJ may order suspension and instalment payment on form N41.

If an application for suspension is made after the warrant has been executed, the court may require that the debtor pay the costs incurred up until that date. If necessary, CCR, Ord 25, r 8(10) permits the court to order sale of all or part of the goods to cover those costs. In this respect, it may be worth noting that some county court bailiffs insist upon making a levy before an N245 application is accepted from the judgment debtor. This is not supported by the CCR as such, but it is clear that part of the motivation for this must be to recoup costs.

If a part warrant was issued and an order is made suspending it on terms, these terms apply to the repayment of the whole balance due under the judgment (CCR, Ord 26, r 11).

4.8.2 Suspension of writs

The same procedure may be followed by a defendant to suspend execution of a writ of *fieri facias*. It may, however, be much more difficult for a person to get a suspension or a variation of terms than in the county court. The High Court does not have the same broad powers to suspend that are granted to the county court by CCA 1981, s 71. See the discussion of stays of execution in the previous chapter at para 3.10.

4.8.3 Withdrawal of warrants

It is possible for the judgment creditor to ask for a warrant of execution to be withdrawn and for possession taken by the bailiff to be abandoned. This is likely to be done in two distinct situations:

- *following an interpleader claim*: this process is described in the next section, but if such a request is received, the court will only require the bailiff to withdraw from possession of those goods and chattels subject to the interpleader claim; and

- *on agreement with the debtor*: it is of course possible for the creditor and debtor to agree terms of payment without the need for the latter to make an application on form N245 for suspension of the warrant. Where this is done, the creditor should ask the court to suspend the warrant. If the debtor subsequently defaults, the creditor can ask for the warrant to be reissued, but it will be treated by the court as a request for the issue of a new warrant of execution (CCR, Ord 26, r 10).

4.9 Interpleader and other claims

The bailiff may inadvertently seize goods which are the property of a third party who is not liable for the debt. In such cases the claimant to the goods may challenge the levy of execution by means of a procedure known as 'interpleader' (see John Kruse, *Law of Seizure of Goods* (Hammicks, 2nd edn, 2009), para 9.26).

4.9.1 County court executions

A written claim to the goods must be filed in the court office and the judgment creditor will then be notified on form N358. The interpleader claimant should act with 'reasonable promptitude' in making such a claim and may be penalised by the court for failing to do so (see *Watson v Park Royal (Caterers) Ltd* [1961] 2 All ER 346 – a delay of 3½ months). The court must require the person making the claim to the goods to provide security based upon the value of the seized items and the bailiff's costs to date. This security then becomes the subject of the court proceedings rather than the goods themselves. If no security is provided, the court will order sale of the goods in question under CCA 1981, s 100(3). The proceeds of sale will be paid into the court to await the outcome of the interpleader claim. If the interpleader claimant's deposit is less than the value of the goods demanded, the county court bailiff will remain in possession or will resume possession of the goods, making periodic checks to ensure that the debtor is taking care of them and that none have been removed.

Once notice of the claim is received by the judgment creditor, 4 days are given to decide whether to admit or dispute it; it is reasonable for an execution creditor to insist that the interpleader claimant provides some details of the basis for the claim. A mere statement of ownership without providing supporting information and/or evidence may be rejected (see *R v Chilton* (1850) 14 QBD 220).

If the third party claim is contested, or if the creditor simply fails to respond in time, a hearing will be arranged by the court and the creditor will receive at least 14 days' notice of the hearing on form N88. At this point the bailiff will be required to withdraw from possession of the goods which have been levied. The security deposit is then the subject matter of the interpleader claim. The execution creditor no longer has a right to seize the goods under dispute – nor has the creditor any right to initiate other enforcement proceedings whilst the matter is pending – though of course another creditor will be able to instruct bailiffs who would then be entitled to try to levy upon the same chattels (remedy now deposit: *Wells v Hughes* [1907] 2 KB 845; creditor cannot seize: *Haddow v Morton* [1894] 1 QB 565; enforcement stayed: *Re Ford* [1886] 18 QBD 369; further distraint: *Cropper v Warner* (1833) Cab & El 152). If the claim is dismissed, the parties will be notified on form N362.

If the claim is admitted on the basis of the evidence supplied by the interpleader claimant, the levy on the goods in question will be cancelled and the bailiff will be ordered to withdraw from possession on form N363.

The interpleader claim can also include a claim for damages by the claimant of the goods. In county court cases under CCR, Ord 33, r 5, within 8 days of receiving the summons, the claimant may enter a claim for any damages s/he feels were incurred as a consequence of the actions of the execution creditor, the bailiff or DJ. The damages claim must be made before the hearing of the interpleader. If it is not, it will be too late afterwards as the decision on the matter by the county court under CCA 1981, s 101 is treated as final and conclusive. Should the claimant forget to claim or to particularise the claim, once the decision has been made the matter cannot be reopened, however well founded the claim for damages.

The court will award damages in any case where it is satisfied that there is the basis for a 'substantial grievance' or that substantial injury has been suffered. Factors to be taken into account when considering an award of damages will include:

- where the bailiff has entered the premises of a stranger and seized goods in belief that they are the debtor's; or
- where the claim arose from the bailiff's own wrongful actions – for instance, goods were seized in the knowledge that they were not the debtor's.

Most grievances will arise as a result of the actions of the county court bailiff, but the claim for damages might be directed against the judgment creditor where s/he has brought about the bailiffs' wrongful acts, for example by directing them to the wrong property or goods.

4.9.2 High Court executions

Interpleader in the High Court follows the same broad procedure as in a county court, but with a few distinctive differences:

- the interpleader claim is served upon the HCEO, who sends the judgment creditor notice of the fact on form PF23. A response from the creditor is required on form PF24 within 7 days;
- the HCEO applies for interpleader depending on the creditor's response. Once the proceedings are initiated, the interpleader claimant must serve on the parties a witness statement or affidavit specifying the goods involved and the basis for the claim;
- the High Court may require payment of security or may order sale of the goods (CPR, Sch 1: RSC, Ord 17, r 6);
- in the High Court any claim for damages will be made separately from the interpleader proceedings.

Depending upon the outcome of any hearing, a number of practice forms exist to serve notice upon the parties. Form PF28 is sent if the claim failed; form PF29 notifies the claimant that the HCEO has been ordered to withdraw. If the claim needs to be set down for trial, the court may issue form PF31 instructing the HCEO to sell the goods in question, form PF32 requires the HCEO to withdraw from possession whilst the matter is pending, and form PF34 notifies the parties of the outcome if the court deals with the claim in a summary manner.

4.9.3 Exempt goods

The interpleader procedure may also be used by the judgment debtor in order to challenge levies upon goods which s/he feels should be regarded as basic exempt items (see para 4.5.3).

4.10 Rent and other claims

Landlords are given priority rights to claim payment of any rent arrears in the execution of judgments. These rights arise under Landlord and Tenant Act 1709, s 1 in the High Court and CCA 1981, s 102 for county courts.

- *Restrictions on claim*: the extent of the rent that may be claimed in priority to the claims of the execution creditor is limited:
  - the landlord is entitled to receive no more than four times any term's rent where the term is less than one year (Execution Act 1844, s 1) subject to a maximum of one year's rent;
  - the rent arrears claimed for must be due under an ongoing landlord and tenant relationship; and

- the landlord can only claim for the rent arrears which are due at the time of seizure. A claim for any sums accruing after the date of the seizure is barred, although if the rent is payable in advance and has fallen due, it is recoverable.

There are also limits as to the seizures against which the landlord may claim:

- the execution cannot be one on a judgment for the landlord; and
- the claim can only be made against one execution even if two are levied.

- *Bailiff's duties*: the bailiff is under no liability to enquire as to the existence of rent arrears or keep the goods in case such a claim emerges. However, if notice of a claim is received it should be investigated. Knowledge of the existence of rent arrears is sufficient notice to the bailiff.

- *Judgment creditor's duties*: although the bailiff is liable to make payment to the landlord, and may face a claim if this is not done, it does not seem to be the case that the execution creditor is also liable.

- *Landlord's duties*: a levy of execution will mean that the landlord cannot then exercise his right of distress for rent as the seized goods are in the custody of the law. To attempt to do so would constitute a trespass against the execution creditor. The landlord cannot insist on sale of the goods but s/he can issue a claim if payment is not made out of the proceeds of sale. The landlord cannot issue a claim for the rent arrears outstanding against the execution creditor and cannot interplead against the seizure.

4.10.1 Procedure in county courts

Under CCA 1981, s 102(2) the landlord may within 5 days of seizure, or before removal of the goods, deliver a written claim stating the rent due and the period to which it applies. The bailiff should then levy for the rent and costs as well as the judgment debt which is already being enforced and should not sell any of the goods within a further five day period unless they are perishable or unless the tenant has requested their sale. Upon sale the bailiff will satisfy the sums due in the following order:

- firstly, the costs of the sale;
- then the landlord's claim not exceeding:
  - 4 weeks rent where the rent is due weekly; or
  - two terms of payment where the letting is on any term of less than a year; or

- otherwise, one year's rent; and
- the sum for which the warrant was issued.

Any surplus or left over goods are returned to the debtor. The cost of the levy for the rent will be calculated on the same basis as any execution and no extra fees may be added.

4.10.2 Procedure in the High Court

A similar procedure is followed by the HCEO except that there must be removal of goods off the premises for Landlord and Tenant Act 1709, s 1 to apply – simply seizing and impounding the goods on the premises by means of a walking possession agreement for the goods will not suffice. If only a portion of goods seized have been removed, the section will also not apply. However, if there is no removal within a reasonable time, the HCEO's rights under the levy will lapse and the landlord will be able to distrain as normal. If the HCEO seizes and sells the goods without physical removal the claim under the 1709 Act will once again not be effective.

In the High Court the claim is for up to one year's rent in total (unlike county courts) and once the maximum is paid the levy may proceed as normal. The HCEO can seize enough to cover the rent plus the judgment debt on receiving notice from the landlord within 5 days of the levy. When the rent claim is received by the HCEO the execution creditor is notified and is required to pay the rent due to the HCEO. If this is not done, the HCEO will withdraw from possession of the goods on the demised premises and will try to levy only on other goods located elsewhere. The subsequent levy by the HCEO will be for both the debt due to the claimant and the rent arrears that they have been obliged to discharge.

4.10.3 Crown claims

Finally, it should be recalled the Crown creditors have priority in levies of execution. If HM Revenue and Customs choose to levy distraint for arrears of income tax or VAT and other indirect taxes, these claims will have preference over any pre-existing levy for a judgment debt. The Crown's claim to priority is only defeated if the execution has proceeded to sale.

In none of the situations described in this section is there is any automatic opportunity for the execution creditor to dispute the claim (unlike interpleader) and a specific application to this effect would have to be made.

4.11 Negligence by the bailiff

If the claimant is dissatisfied with the steps taken to levy the warrant or writ, it may be possible to take action to recover compensation. County Courts Act 1984, s 124 allows an aggrieved party to make complaint to a judge where it is felt that an opportunity to levy was lost through neglect, connivance or omission on the part of the county court bailiff.

The bailiff will be summonsed to appear at a hearing by issue of form N336 under CPR, Sch 2: CCR, Ord 34, r 1. At the hearing the judge can order the bailiff to pay damages for the loss sustained by the claimant, although these shall not exceed the sum for which the warrant was issued. County Courts Act 1984, s 123 also imposes upon DJs a general responsibility for the acts and defaults of court bailiffs.

Similar claims may be made against HCEOs. Damages may be recovered for negligence, delay or a complete failure to levy (see *Re Essex Sheriff, Terrell v Fisher* (1862) 10 WR 796; *Pitcher v King* (1844) 5 QB 758).

Execution against Goods

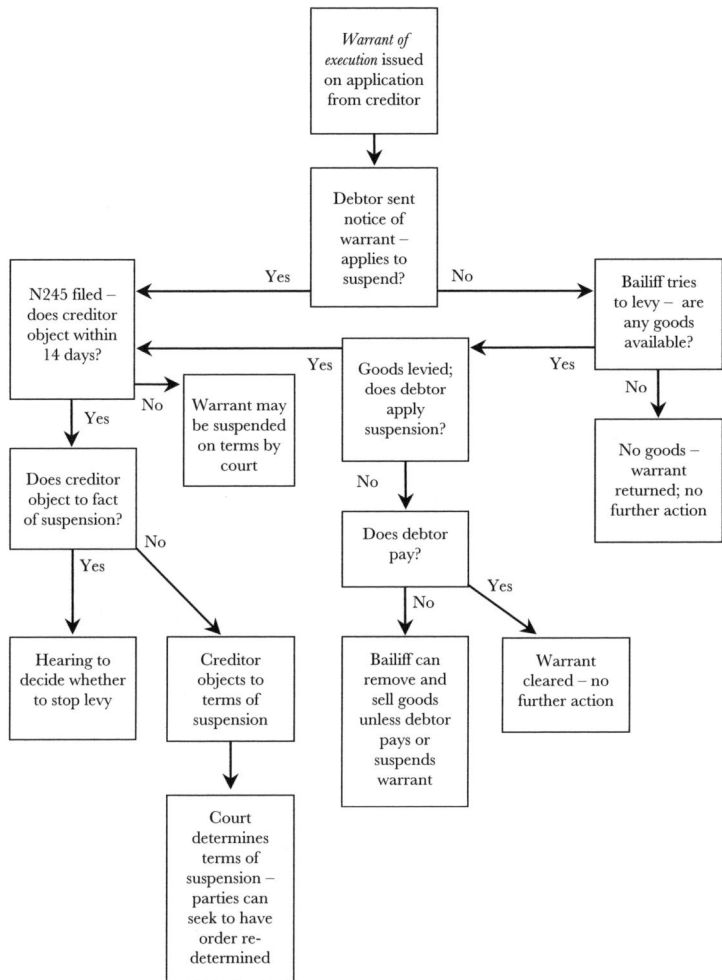

Figure 4.1: Warrants of execution

5 Attachment of Earnings Orders

5.1 Introduction

An attachment of earnings order (AEO) offers a judgment creditor the hope of a guaranteed regular payment of the judgment debt by the judgment debtor's employers on the debtor's behalf. Success will depend particularly upon the information available about the debtor and proper preparation is again essential. Figure 5.1 (see p 97) outlines the attachment of earnings procedure.

There are a number of key considerations to bear in mind before proceeding with an application for an AEO:

- *Is the debtor employed?* Only earnings from employment (including statutory sick pay) may be attached, therefore a self-employed individual cannot be reached this way. If there is any doubt whether particular payments to a judgment debtor qualify as 'earnings', application may be made to the county court under Attachment of Earnings Act 1971 (AEA 1971), s 16 and CPR, Sch 2: CCR, Ord 27, r 11. Such an application may be made by the employer, the debtor or the judgment creditor. A hearing date will be fixed and notice given to the relevant parties. Normally application is made by the party who is making periodical payments to the debtor in response to the receipt from the court of an AEO, but there is no reason why a judgment creditor should not seek a determination and clarification from the court (see *Edmonds v Edmonds* [1965] 1 WLR 58 – application by trustees of a pension fund).

- *Is the employment full time?* The court must take personal expenses into consideration (see para 5.4.1) so that, if the income is too low, it may not be feasible or worthwhile seeking an AEO.

- *Is the debtor unemployed?* Benefits cannot be attached. However note that, although a state retirement pension is not attachable, a former employer's occupational pension counts as earnings and may be attached.

- *Is the employment stable?* If the person is in agency work, with periods without work, or if they have spells of unemployment for other reasons, it will make the AEO very difficult to administer.

- *Are there other debts?* The request for an AEO may precipitate the making of an administration order which is attached to the debtor's earnings. An administration order may also be attached to earnings when it is first made on a debtor's application or later in response to a default in payments by the debtor (see Chapter 3 and AEA 1971, ss 4 and 5).

In order to decide whether spending the money on an application for an AEO is worthwhile, ascertaining whether or not the debtor is employed is plainly the key question for the claimant. There are a number of sources of information which might be used:

- previous information gathered in the course of business dealings with the individual;

- information supplied by the debtor earlier in the court proceedings – for example on admission form N9A or on application to vary judgment or suspend a bailiff's warrant on form N245;

- the evidence produced by an oral examination (see Chapter 3);

- the results of a search of the court's register of attachments (see para 5.2.2); or

- information gathered in the course of debt collection contacts with a debtor. Daytime calls postponed because the individual is out at work will give the claimant some confidence in an application – though the person may of course be self-employed.

To summarise, AEOs are potentially a very effective means of guaranteed recovery, if the right preconditions are satisfied. If wages exist they will be attached – and for creditors the order is very cheap to operate once established as all the administration will be carried out by the employer and the court. However, the procedure can be lengthy, attachments can be disrupted by other court orders, low wages may render it ineffective or the debtor may deliberately seek to evade the order by giving up work.

A county court has the power to make an attachment of earnings order under AEA 1971, s 1(2)(b) and CPR, Sch 2: CCR, Ord 27. High Court judgments cannot be enforced by an AEO in the High Court, but will have to be transferred to a county court for recovery in this manner (see para 5.2.2).

5.2 Application

Application for an attachment of earnings order may be made by any creditor with an enforceable judgment (see below) or by any creditor included in an administration order (see para 3.3.3).

5.2.1 Definition of earnings

The earnings which may be attached by such an application are defined in AEA 1971, s 23. These include:

- wages or salary, which will include all fees, bonuses, commission, overtime and other payments paid to the individual under their contract of employment. Earnings paid in advance, such as holiday pay, will be attachable, as will backdated payments of wages;
- pensions and payments made in compensation of loss of employment; and
- statutory sick pay.

Deductions may only be taken from these sums after allowance has been made for payments of income tax, class 1 national insurance contributions and superannuation payments or pension contributions.

Payments made to debtors which are not attachable by an AEO include:

- pay to members of the armed forces;
- pay to employees of the Northern Ireland government;
- statutory maternity pay, paternity pay and adoption pay;
- tax credits;
- guaranteed minimum pension;
- seaman's wages;
- social security benefits; and
- disability pensions. A disability pension may be distinguished from an 'ill-health pension'. The latter was held attachable as the level of payment was calculated by reference to years of service with the employer rather than by extent of disability (see *Miles v Miles* [1979] 1 WLR 371).

As mentioned in para 5.1, if there is any dispute about the nature of remuneration received by the debtor, this question may be resolved by the court upon application from a concerned party.

5.2.2 Application procedure

Application for an order is made to the debtor's local court or, where the debtor does not live in England and Wales or the creditor does not know the judgment debtor's current home address at all, the application can be made to the court where judgment was entered. If AEOs are sought against two or more debtors jointly liable under a judgment, any county court in whose areas one of those debtors resides is appropriate. If one of these is the court in which the judgment was entered, this should be used.

To be able to make an application, there must be a debt or instalment of at least £50 due (CCR, Ord 27, r 7(9)). The request for an order is normally made on form N337 certifying the balance and arrears due on the judgment, though it may also be done by supplying the court with two completed copies of the notice to be served upon the debtor (form N55). A fee, currently £100, is payable.

If a High Court judgment is to be enforced, it will be necessary for the judgment creditor to transfer the case to a county court. The High Court may make an order transferring the judgment under CPR, r 70.3. Application must then be made to the appropriate county court supplying the following information:

- a copy of the judgment or order;

- a certificate verifying the amount due under the judgment;

- if a writ of execution has previously been issued in the High Court, a copy of the return from the HCEO; and

- a copy of the High Court's order transferring the case to a county court (CPR, Part 70, PD 3.1).

5.2.3 Attachments register

Under CCR, Ord 27, r 2 every county court keeps a register of debtors within that court's area against whom AEOs are in force. This includes not just orders made by that court but orders made in any other county court, as it is the duty of each court office to notify the court in whose area a debtor lives when an AEO is made against him/her. The High Court is also notified of AEOs made on transferred High Court judgments.

Before submitting an application the creditor can request a search of the court's index of existing attachments to see whether any other orders are in place. This is done by completing form N336; no fee is payable. It is worthwhile conducting such a search as some AEOs have priority over others: those for maintenance or fines are paid before those for judgment debts, and the latter are paid by the employer in chronological order, so the search may save the claimant a wasted fee if there are already too many creditors ahead of them in the queue for surplus income. All the same, a search of the register is not comprehensive. The problem is that, whilst orders made in the magistrates' courts and the High Court will be notified and recorded, deductions ordered by the Child Support Agency and by the local authority for council tax arrears will not appear but may have priority (see below).

5.3 Disclosure of means

Fundamental to the making of an AEO is the acquisition by the court of information on the debtor's employment and remuneration. The court is provided with a several stage process and progressively more serious sanctions in order to be able to obtain this.

5.3.1 Initial notices

Notice of the application is issued to the debtor on form N55 with reply form N56 attached. Form N56 is a statement of income and expenditure and should be returned to the court by the defendant within 8 days. If the requisite details are available, under CCR, Ord 27, r 6 the court may also send the employer a form (N338) to complete which provides a statement of the debtor's current and anticipated earnings. This power may be exercised by the court at any stage in the proceedings. If the named employers do not have the judgment debtor in their employment, the court must be notified by them within 10 days (AEA 1971, s 7(2)).

If the judgment debtor fails to clear the debt or to reply on form N56, the court prepares form N61 ordering the defendant to supply the statement of means within a further 8 days. S/he will be notified of the court's powers under AEA 1971, s 14 to order that this information is supplied by either the debtor or the debtor's employer and that it can be treated an offence under AEA 1971, s 23 to fail to comply. Proceedings will only be taken in connection with the offence if the documents were served personally or the court is satisfied that they came to the person's attention in time (CCR, Ord 27, r 7A and Ord 29). This notice warns the debtor of the consequences of failing to comply and also instructs him/her to make all future payments on the judgment debt to the court rather than the judgment creditor. This is served either personally by the bailiff or by the creditor. The employer can also be ordered to comply on form N16A.

Sanctions exist under AEA 1971, s 23 for failure by either the debtor or the employer to supply information as required or for supplying false information. The penalty is a fine of up to level 2 on summary conviction in a magistrates' court or a fine of £250 and/or committal for up to 14 days imposed by a county court judge. Allegations of offences under the Act will be dealt with at a hearing unless the court decides to proceed summarily. The summons is issued on form N62 and once again must be served personally by the claimant or court bailiff.

5.3.2 Notices to show cause

If the debtor still refuses to comply, form N63 is issued, requiring the debtor to show cause at a hearing why a committal order should not be made against him/her. This notice gives at least 5 days' warning of the hearing and is likely to be served personally by the bailiff. If the debtor does not comply even at this stage by supplying the necessary personal information, a fine or committal to prison for up to 14 days may be ordered by the court under AEA 1971, s 23(3). Committal will be suspended and an attachment order made on form N118 provided that the debtor attends court and completes form N56. If a suspended committal order is made, the debtor may apply to extend the period of suspension by attending the court or by submitting a written request. This application will have to be supported by a statement of the reasons for failing to comply with the original terms of the suspension. The court will then arrange a hearing of the application and will give 3 days' notice to the parties.

In practice, if committal is contemplated the normal procedure will often be for the court to issue an arrest warrant on form N112A under AEA 1971, s 23(1A). This will require the county court bailiff to call early in the day upon the judgment debtor in order to bring him/her into the court preparatory to appearing before the judge. The person will be held in the court awaiting their appearance and will be given a final opportunity to complete form N56. Readers will not be surprised to learn that, at this stage in the enforcement process, there is usually a very high level of compliance on the part of judgment debtors, but if the person still does not co-operate, a committal warrant will be issued on form N59.

5.4 Making orders

When the debtor replies to the application and supplies details of means to the court, a copy must be supplied to the judgment creditor. AEOs may be made by court staff or by judicial staff. The amount of evidence

Attachment of Earnings Orders

available will be the determining factor; the court officer will proceed immediately to make an order if s/he feels enough information has been supplied by the debtor on the reply form.

5.4.1 Court officers

Initially the court staff will set the rate of payment based upon the information supplied upon form N56 and using a standard calculator (form EX119). The debtor is granted an allowance for his/her basic needs in the form of a 'protected earnings rate' (PER). This is the minimum figure of wages below which income may not be reduced by the AEO. If wages fell below this level for one week or month, for example, no attachment could be taken by the employer. This provision gives orders the flexibility necessary to cope with wages that fluctuate from week to week or month to month by allowing court staff to set an average minimum figure (see *R v York Magistrates Court ex parte Grimes* (1997) 161 JP 550; however, note the case of *Cross v Cross* (1997) CO/4291/96 in which the defendant was director of the company of which he was employee, which enabled him to manipulate his earnings so as to defeat the AEO).

The court staff use the Income Support rates as guidance to personal needs allowances when calculating the level of the PER, with additional allowances being made for housing costs, essential work-related expenses and for the payment of other court orders. The advantage of this protected figure is that it should ensure the debtor's ability to meet ongoing liabilities such as housing costs so that the creditor should not lose trace of the person. If the court calculates that the debtor's total household income (including any income received by partners and spouses but ignoring disability benefits) is less than the PER, no AEO will be made.

5.4.2 District judges

If the court staff feel unable to make an order based on the information they have, the matter is referred to a DJ who may make an order without a hearing if s/he feels able, or alternatively may summons the parties to a hearing at which the debtor's means are explored. The parties get at least 8 days' notice of this. If the judgment creditor does not appear at the hearing but has sent the court a witness statement or affidavit of evidence, or has asked for the hearing to proceed in his absence, the court will hear the application and make a decision. The court also has the power to make an administration order at this point (see para 3.2.2 and AEA 1971, s 4). The administration order may be attached to earnings or the AEO may be discharged by the court on making the administration order.

The AEO will be made on form N60 and copies are sent to the claimant, defendant and employer. The AEO will include costs incurred by the judgment creditor – for example, for a solicitor attending a hearing, preparing a witness statement and serving an application or for counsel's appearance where the court has allowed this. The order identifies the debtor by his/her name and address, place of work, job title and works number. If, on receipt of the AEO, the employers advise the court that the debtor is not in their employment, the order will be discharged. If the AEO is reissued after a change of employment, the court will make the necessary changes to the personal information it contains.

As described before, either side may ask for a determination to be reconsidered if they are unhappy with the rate of payment ordered or any other aspect of the AEO. Such a request should be made within 14 days of the making of the AEO. The request is made on form N244 and the parties will receive at least 2 days' notice of the hearing which is arranged. At such a hearing the DJ may confirm the terms of the existing AEO or may set it aside and a substitute a new order.

If the debtor fails to attend the hearing before the DJ it will be adjourned under AEA 1971, s 23(1) and notice of the date of the adjourned hearing will be served on form N63. If, then, the debtor fails to attend or refuses to answer questions, s/he may be committed, may have a suspended committal order made against him/her or may be arrested and brought before the court (form N112A). At this point, if form N56 is completed, any committal order should be discharged. If the defendant will still not co-operate, committal of up to 14 days may be ordered on form N59.

An AEO can be varied or discharged by the court subsequently. This may be done for a variety of reasons (see below). Notice is usually given to the parties on form N341 but the court may dispense with a hearing if it thinks this is unnecessary (CCR, Ord 27, r 13(9)).

5.5 Payment

A rate of payment known as the 'normal deduction rate' (NDR) is notified to the employer so that deductions from wages may begin on the first pay day following the date notice is received. The NDR is a percentage of the surplus left after the PER has been allowed for – normally a half to two thirds of the surplus is taken. If earnings fall below the protected level in one week, no deduction will be taken. Missed payments are not carried forward to be taken in subsequent weeks; there will simply be a sanctioned non-payment by the debtor for that period.

Under AEA 1971, ss 6 and 7, employers must comply with the AEO, regularly sending money to the court. A charge of £1 may be made to the debtor every time a deduction is taken from his/her wages. Deductions will of course cease once the attached judgment has been discharged and the court is obliged to notify the employer when an AEO ends. Where an employer goes into liquidation before a judgment debt has been discharged – and especially where the employer's insolvency means that not all deductions are paid over to the court – this will prevent the debtor from seeking a certificate of satisfaction of the judgment. This is because the order is only effective in reducing the debts when payment is received by the creditor (see *Whibley v Cross* [1976] CLY 2108, Wandsworth County Court).

Strict duties are laid down for employers and employees to ensure that a debtor cannot evade an order. Generally, employers have an obligation to take all reasonable steps to comply with an order. More specifically, there are requirements for the court to be told within 10 days if the employee leaves his/her employer (AEA 1971, s 7(2)), for a person to tell a new employer about their status and for the employer then to notify the court of the fact of the debtor's appointment within 7 days (s 9(4)). The court must be notified of all changes in employment by both the debtor and the employer and failure to comply with any of these can be treated as an offence for which a fine or imprisonment may be imposed (AEA 1971, ss 15 and 23).

Whilst an AEO is in place, other enforcement of the judgment debt is inhibited (AEA 1971, s 8). Permission of the court can be given to allow execution upon goods but the attachment may at the same time be cancelled by the court (CCR, Ord 27, r 13(8)). An order can be varied on application from the debtor under AEA 1971, s 9 where there is a change in circumstances such as a drop in income.

5.6 Complications

There are a number of potential complications to AEOs, which may be encountered during the application for or the currency of an order.

5.6.1 Priority

The first problem is that if other orders are already in place these can have priority, especially if they are for fines or maintenance. Employers are required to deal with attachments for judgments on a chronological basis, so far as there is income available above the PER (AEA 1971, Sch 3). Attachments for unpaid council tax/business rates also have priority over those for judgment debts. If the court later makes an AEO for a debt with priority to the judgment debt, it can vary or discharge the earlier order if it considers this to be necessary.

5.6.2 Suspended orders

The debtor may make a request on form N56 for the AEO to be suspended by the court. If the court is convinced that the person's employment might be threatened by the making of an AEO, and by the employer finding out about the debtor's indebtedness, it may exercise its general powers under CCA 1981, s 71 to make an AEO but to suspend its actual implementation using form N64. In other words, the debtor has a last chance to make payments voluntarily but, if payments are missed, the employer will be notified. If an AEO is already in place, a suspended order will not be made. If payments cease, the creditor may complete form N446 asking that the employer be served with the order. There is no fee for submitting this form to the court.

A judgment creditor might oppose the suspension of the order on a number of grounds:

- *the nature of the debtor's employment*: a request for suspension may be argued to be unnecessary because of the identity of the debtor's employer (for example a very large company or public body which would be unlikely to dismiss an individual because of an attachment) or because of the length of the person's employment (in which case there would be protection from unfair dismissal); or

- *the debtor's past record*: alternatively, if the debtor has a history of making offers to pay which have not been met, or has generally sought to avoid or evade enforcement, the court may be persuaded that suspension is not appropriate.

The opportunity to make such representations would arise upon receiving notification of the making of the AEO. A redetermination of the term of the order suspending its effect could be requested (see para 5.4.2).

5.6.3 Changes in circumstances

Under AEA 1971, s 9 the court has the power of its own motion to vary, suspend or even discharge the order where the defendant's circumstances change, but the parties may be given an opportunity to object to the order. If an attachment is varied, the employer must implement it within 7 days.

5.6.4 Unemployment

The fourth problem is if the debtor loses his or her job. The AEO is not cancelled but goes into abeyance until further attachable earnings become available (AEA 1971, s 9). If the creditor wishes to seek other means of recovery after the debtor became unemployed, it would be necessary to have the AEO discharged first.

5.6.5 Members of the armed forces

Under AEA 1971, s 24(2) a county court may not make an AEO against either the pay or the allowances of a member of the armed forces. Instead, under Army Act 1955, s 151A, a similar deduction may be made by an authorised officer. This is a discretionary power, but deductions may be made for liabilities incurred before the person joined the services.

5.6.6 Administration orders

As has been mentioned, on an application for an AEO the court may decide to make an administration order to consolidate the defendant's outstanding debts or may order the debtor to provide a list of his/her creditors with a view to making an administration order. This may lead to discharge of any AEO in force – alternatively the court may secure payment of the administration order by this means.

5.6.7 Consolidated orders

One of the parties may seek to have a consolidated order made under AEA 1971, s 17 and CPR, Sch 2: CCR, Ord 27, rr 18–22. A creditor may apply under r 19(1)(b), though it is very difficult to see what benefit this would have. An employer may also seek a consolidated AEO if asked to administer two or more orders (r 19(4)). The court may also make a consolidated order of its own motion if it receives a request for an AEO to be made against a judgment debtor who is already subject to an AEO (r 20). Lastly, if there are already other attachments in place, they may all be consolidated into one attachment of earnings order on application by the debtor. This may make sense for the defendant, particularly as it would save upon the £1 administration fee taken by the employer for each AEO. It should however be mentioned that, where the court administers a consolidated order, it deducts 10p in every £1 distributed to creditors to cover its administrative expenses. It may mean, though, that each creditor receives a much lower rate of repayment once the court views the debtor's financial problems as a whole. Also, as mentioned already, an administration order may be made.

If the debtor requests a consolidated order, the matter will be transferred to the county court which made the original AEO. The parties who may be affected by a consolidated order will be notified of the application on form N66A and are asked to give the court notice of any objections they may have to the proposed order within 14 days. If no objections are received, the consolidated order will be made. If an objection is made, the matter is referred to a DJ who will consider the reasons for the objection and will decide whether or not to make the consolidated order.

Once a consolidated AEO has been made on form N66, another judgment creditor may apply to be incorporated within it (r 21). Again, unless the judgment creditor has surplus income substantially in excess of his/her needs, it is difficult to see the advantage of this.

The court receives payments from the employer under the consolidated order. These sums are distributed pro-rata between the judgment creditors and dividends may 'from time to time be declared and distributed' by the court office (r 22). The court normally waits until 10% of the debt has been received before declaring a dividend to creditors.

5.7 Monitoring

All attachments are handled centrally through the Centralised Attachment of Earnings System (which is administered from Northampton County Court). This office conducts regular monitoring of AEOs to ensure that payments are made and to follow up those orders where payment is not received with both the debtor and the employer. It should be noted, however, that consolidated orders and administration orders with attachments are paid to the local court.

In conclusion, as has been seen, AEOs have significant drawbacks as well as benefits. Regular payment may be ensured at low cost, but the orders may be undermined or their value diminished in a number of ways. Additionally, it is possible for debtors to use orders for their own advantage in situations where they have existing multiple debt problems.

Attachment of Earnings Orders

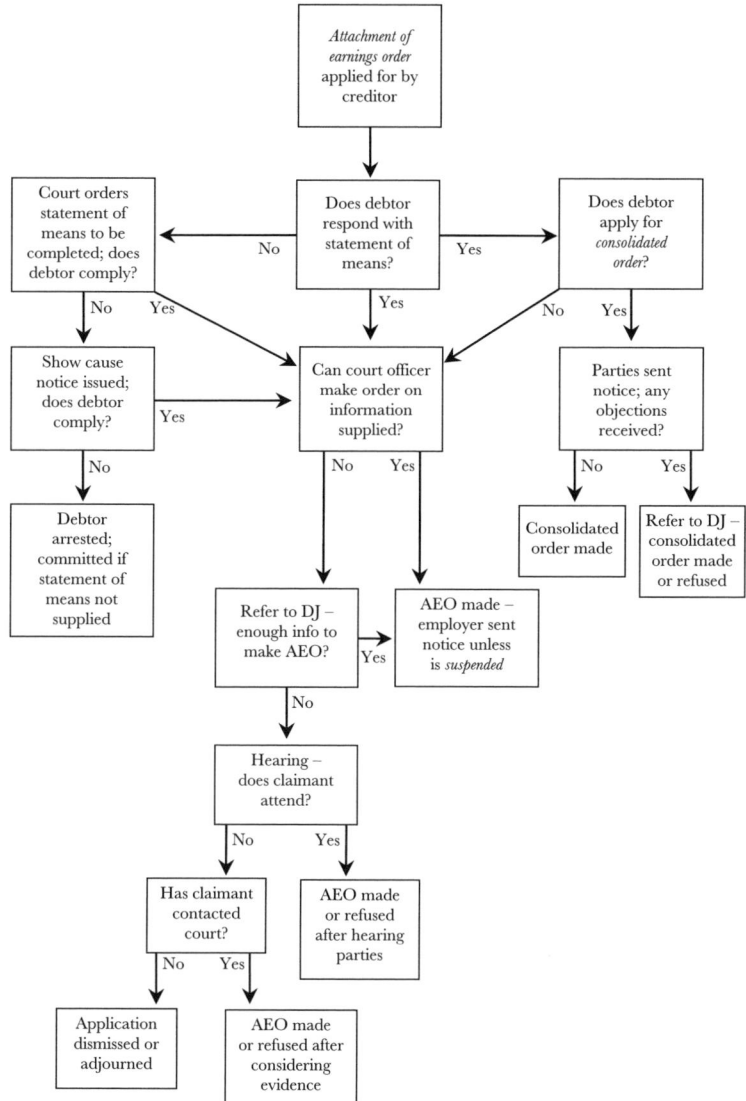

Figure 5.1: Attachment of earnings orders

6 Third Party Debt Orders

6.1 Introduction

This procedure was formerly known as the 'garnishee order' and is a means of collecting any debt, or at least a proportion of it, which is 'due or accruing due' to the debtor from a third party. This may involve payment from the judgment debtor's bank account or from a person (whether an individual, partnership or company) who owes money to the debtor. The third party debtor must be within the jurisdiction of the court, in England and Wales, and a relationship of creditor and debtor must exist between the judgment debtor and third party. That said, provided that the third party is within the jurisdiction, it does not matter that the debt in the account is in a foreign currency – it may still be attached (see *Choice Investments Ltd v Jeromnimom, Midland Bank Ltd, garnishees* [1981] QB 149). For the liability to be attachable, the debt must be such that the debtor him/herself could enforce it by court proceedings (see *Richardson v Richardson* [1927] P 228; *Beasly v Roney* [1891] 1 QB 509).

The power to make such an order arises under CCA 1981, s 108, Senior Courts Act 1981 (SCA 1981), s 40 and CPR, Part 72. Just as with charging orders, a third party debt order is a form of execution and may only be initiated where there has been default upon payment of the judgment debt. If instalments are being maintained in line with the court order, no application may be made to the court (see *White, Son & Pill v Stennings* [1911] 2 KB 418).

6.2 Attachable debts

Because the third party debt order procedure is 'paper based and fairly mechanistic' and because its impact upon a third party can be potentially 'drastic', it is only intended to apply to debts owed in the name of the judgment debtor. Although in principle the court could protect a third party by requiring cross-undertakings, in other or more complex cases the appointment of a receiver or the making of a charging order would usually be more appropriate ways to proceed (see *Continental Transfert Technique Ltd v Federal Government of Nigeria & Others* [2009] EWHC 2898 (Comm)).

The judgment creditor may, therefore, attach the following:

- current accounts;
- savings accounts;
- debts payable by instalments to the judgment debtor, which will presumably include judgment debts (see *Tapp v Jones* [1875] 10 QB 591);
- a debt due under a dishonoured cheque given to the judgment debtor by the third party;
- money due to a partner from the firm;
- rent due to the judgment debtor from a tenant (see *Mitchell v Lee* [1867] 2 QB 259);
- money held by a solicitor or HCEO in respect of the judgment debtor; and
- other debts, such as sums due under an endowment policy.

The case authorities also permit us to identify a number of non-attachable debts. These include:

- unliquidated damages (see *Johnson v Diamond* (1855) 11 Exch 73);
- sums held by a court on behalf of a judgment debtor, although the execution creditor may apply for an order that these are paid over (see para 6.9);
- debts owned jointly to the judgment debtor and a third party (see *Macdonald v Tacquah Goldmines Co* [1884] 13 QBD 535);
- sums paid into the debtor's account on behalf of a third party, whether that person is a spouse or some other individual (see *Hirschhorn v Evans* [1938] 3 All ER 491);
- sums paid by the debtor into a spouse's or partner's account for the purposes of providing a housekeeping allowance (see *Harrods Ltd v Tester* [1937] 2 All ER 236, CA);
- funds in the hands of some court officer other than a bailiff, such as the Official Receiver, liquidator or police officer;
- sums due to be paid under a will (see *Lansforsakringar Bank AB v Wood* [2007] EWHC 2419 (QB));
- an educational grant paid to a student (this will presumably apply to bursaries and educational maintenance allowances today) (see *Macdonald & Co v Davy* (1981) CLY 350);
- money due under a pension;
- money held in a bank to the account of a trustee;

Third Party Debt Orders

- the agreement of an insurance company to indemnify the debtor for a damages liability;

- a liability which *may* become due, but which is not certain. If a debt depends upon accounts being prepared and disputes being arbitrated, it is treated as contingent only and cannot be attachable (see *Kier Regional Ltd v City & General (Holborn) Ltd & Others* [2008] EWHC 2454 (TCC));

- future debts, instead a receiver may be appointed under CPR, Part 69 or a charging order could be made (see *Bagnall v Carlton* [1877] 6 Ch D 130; *Soinco SACI v Novokuznetsk Aluminium Plant* [1998] QB 406), see Chapter 7; and

- salary accruing but not actually due (see *Hall v Pritchett* [1877] 3 QBD 215).

As the sample in the above lists indicates, a wide range of liabilities may be attached by third party debt order. Even so, the vast majority of orders made affect bank accounts. Once again this is for simple reasons of the information available to the creditor. If a claimant becomes aware of other potentially attachable sums, whether through investigation or sheer good luck, a specialist text should be consulted to establish whether a third party debt order can apply (see for example *Halsbury's Laws of England* (Lexis Nexis), vol 17 'Execution' or *Civil Court Practice* (Butterworths)).

If the claimant has all the relevant details and there is the money available, the third party debt order can be very effective, prompt and inexpensive. It will prove to be a waste of time and money if there is either no account or no money in it and, of course, the reduction in income for the relevant period or a loss of savings may prejudice the debtor's ability to make further instalment payments if the whole debt is not cleared by the one attachment.

6.3 Preconditions

For an order to be successful in attaching an account, the defendant must have both an account and money in it at the time when the application is made and the claimant needs to know either details of the bank, branch, account number. Alternatively, the judgment creditor will need to have uncovered details of debtors of the judgment debtor. Timing will be an important factor. For instance, in seeking to attach a current account, an application at the end of the month after the defendant has been paid is more likely to succeed than one made midway through the month.

A preliminary to an application for an order will often need to be an examination as the debtor's means, as described in Chapter 3, but it may be the case that the creditor already has some banking details for the defendant obtained during the course of their previous business relationship.

Although there are clearly attendant problems and risks with a third party debt order, when they do work they can be extremely effective and swift.

6.4 Application

Application for an order is very straightforward once the basic information is known and the preconditions have been met. These require that a minimum of £50 must be outstanding and that the defendant must be in arrears on the judgment. It seems that the Limitation Act 1980 is of no application to requests for third party debt orders and that they may be made at any time after the date of the judgment. It will be up to the debtor to raise issues of delay if s/he feels they are relevant (see *Fellows v Thornton* [1884] 14 QBD 335; *Westacre Investments Inc v Yugoimport SDPR* [2008] EWHC 801 (Comm); *Yorkshire Bank Finance v Mulhall* [2008] EWCA Civ 1156, para 24).

The claimant must complete application form N349 providing the following information:

- details of the judgment debt, the extent of the debtor's default upon any instalment payments due under the court's payment order and the amounts remaining unpaid under the judgment;

- the details of the debt owed by the third party and of any bank or building society account to be attached. If only partial information is in the creditor's possession, this must be disclosed to the court;

- confirmation that the identified third party is within England and Wales and is indebted to the judgment debtor; and

- the details (if known) of any other person who might have a claim to the debt to be attached.

This application is filed at the court where judgment was entered (unless the case has been transferred to a different county court) with the fee (currently £100). Applicants are warned in the practice direction to CPR, Part 72 that the court will not grant speculative applications. Interim orders will only be made if the application includes evidence to back up the statement that a debt or account exists. The sources and grounds for the information provided to the court must be disclosed. If there have been previous attempts to enforce the judgment by means of a third party debt order – or concurrent applications are in existence – this must be disclosed in the application for the interim order.

6.5 Interim order

The application is then considered by a DJ and an interim order will be made if the court is satisfied that sufficient evidence has been supplied of the probable existence of an account in the name of the judgment debtor (and this statement may be based on evidence that is a year or more old). It is not necessary for the creditor to demonstrate that there are actually funds available in the account as the court will accept the practical impossibility of confirming this (see *Alawiye & Anglo-Arabic Graphics Ltd v Mahmood & National Westminster Bank plc*, ChD, 23 February 2006, unreported).

If an interim order is made specifying the sum due under the judgment along with the creditor's fixed costs for making the application (see para 1.3.2) The order is sent to the third party on form N84 giving not less than 21 days' notice of the hearing date. If the defendant's debtor is a bank, or other financial institution, service on the third party will be at their head or registered office, but a copy may be sent to the relevant branch as well. It should be noted that service of form N84 on the judgment debtor takes place at least 7 days before the hearing date, but at least 7 days after service upon the third party. This of course prevents the defendant emptying the relevant account and defeating the creditor. The order may be served either by the court or by the judgment creditor. If the latter takes on the responsibility, a certificate of service (form N215) must be filed in court not less than 2 days before the hearing of the final order and must be produced to the judge at the hearing.

On receipt of the interim order it is the duty of any bank or building society to carry out a search for all accounts in the name of the judgment debtor. The third party's further duty is to freeze these accounts so as to ensure that the balance does not fall below the amount specified in the order and to give details of the account number(s) and the balance(s) if the account is in credit and of any right of set-off claimed against the account(s) to the court and the judgment creditor within 7 days of service of the order. Under CCA 1981, s 109 the financial institution may make a charge to the debtor's account to cover its expenses in doing this, regardless of the balance of the account. The charges made by the bank to the customer's account should not exceed £55 in total (see Attachment of Debts (Expenses) Order 1996 (SI 1996/3098)). If the account attached is held jointly with another person who is not liable for the debt, the third party is not required to give any information about it or to freeze it; this also applies to accounts held by individual partners where the judgment was entered against the partnership. However, if the judgment is against joint debtors, debts due to either may be attached (see *Miller v Mynn* (1859) 1 E&E 1075). If the name stated in the interim order does not exactly match the name of the account holder so as to raise doubts as to whether the correct person has been indentified, the financial institution is entitled not to comply with the order but must inform the court and the judgment creditor of the apparent problem within seven days of service (see *Koch v Mineral Ore Syndicate, London & South Western Bank Ltd, Garnishees* [1910] 54 Sol Jo 600).

In respect of debts owed to the judgment debtor by any other individual, that person's duty is to inform the court within 7 days of receipt of notice of the order whether they deny owing any sums to the judgment debtor or whether that debt is less than the sum to be enforced by the order. If no response is made to the court, it will be assumed that the existence of a liability to the defendant is not denied.

From the time that the third party receives notice the account or debt is frozen – the order is binding upon the third party (CPR, r 72.4) and no money may be withdrawn or paid to the defendant if this means that the balance in the account will be reduced below the level of the amount owed to the judgment creditor. The courts have described the effect of an interim order in these terms: it creates a defeasible charge in favour of the judgment creditor which becomes effective on the making of the final order and gives the creditor priority over other judgment creditors. Money may be paid into the account after the interim order has been made, but these funds will not be affected by the order (see *FG Hemisphere Associates LLC v Congo* [2005] EWHC 3201 (QB) – effect of order; *Heppenstall v Jackson* [1939] 1 KB 585 – payments to account).

6.6 Hearing

Before the hearing, the third party may serve notice that no money is owed to the judgment debtor, either because the account in question is not in credit or because the sum owed by the third party to the judgment debtor is insufficient to clear the amount specified in the interim order (CPR, r 72.8). If the claimant wishes to dispute either statement, written evidence setting out the grounds for this must be filed in court and served on the other parties not less than 3 days before the hearing. If the third party is other than a bank, for example a trade debtor, the court may hear and determine any dispute over liability at the scheduled hearing or may give directions for trial in more complex cases.

If the objection to the order is the existence of another claim to the sum owed, the debtor or the third party are required, at least 3 days before the hearing, to file in court written evidence in the form of a witness statement setting out the grounds for this assertion. Notice will then be served by the court upon this other party. At the scheduled hearing the court will determine any disputes, objections or claims or will give directions for their trial. Finally, note that the whole case can be transferred to a court more convenient to the debtor for hearing if s/he makes application to this effect.

When considering whether to make a final order, the court should take into account all relevant factors, such as the circumstances of the debtor and the position of any other creditors that are known about. The court has the discretion to refuse to make an order final, for a variety of reasons. This may be done, for example, because the debtor is insolvent or because it is thought that other creditors will be unduly prejudiced. If the judgment debtor is not obviously insolvent then the court will be entitled to make the order, even though by so doing it will be preferring one creditor over the others; the fact that one creditor is actively seeking to recover a judgment debt whilst others are not does not render the making of an order unfair to the rest (see *Pritchard v Westminster Bank Ltd* [1969] 1 All ER 999). The court may determine that a debtor is insolvent, in light of other known creditors, even though s/he is not subject to formal insolvency proceedings such as an IVA. The financial institution holding the account being attached is entitled to object on the basis that it is entitled to some or all of the money in the account by way of an equitable charge or a right of set off, but the liability in question must have accrued at the time of service of the interim order. If such a claim exceeds the debt owed to the judgment debtor, the court will exercise its discretion to refuse the third party debt order (see *Fraser v Oystertec plc* [2004] EWHC 1582 (Ch); *Society of Lloyds v Cook*, 16 September 1999, unreported; *Rainbow v Moorgate Properties* [1975] 2 All ER 821; *Sampson v Seaton Railway Co* [1874] 10 QB 28). If a debt exists, but is not yet payable, the order should be made final but payment should be postponed until the debt becomes due (see *O'Driscoll v Manchester Insurance Committee* [1915] 3 KB 499; *Re Cowan's Estate, Rapier v Wright* [1880] 14 Ch D 638). If the debtor is subject to prior claims, this will not prevent an order being made. For example, sums payable under a judgment in favour of the defendant were held to be attachable, even though the litigation which led to the award was publicly funded and the proceeds were therefore subject to the Legal Services Commission statutory charge (see *Beechwood Construction Ltd v Afza & Batty* [2008] EWHC 2671 (Civ)).

Where the third party does not contest the application or where the defendant fails to appear or show cause why the order should not be made final, then at the scheduled a final third party debt order will be made by the court on form N85.

6.7 Hardship payment orders

If, because of the making of an interim order, a debtor finds that s/he and his/her household is suffering 'hardship in meeting ordinary living expenses' as a result of not being able to withdraw money from the frozen account, s/he can seek a 'hardship payment order' from the local court.

Application is made to the relevant court on form N244 supported by written evidence of the difficulties and the need for payment to be released. The debtor must prove his/her desperate financial position by supplying the court with documentary evidence such as bank statements, wage slips, tenancy agreements or mortgage statements.

At least 2 days' notice of a hearing of this application is given to the creditor, although a hearing before a DJ may be dispensed with by the court in cases of 'exceptional urgency'. Nonetheless, the court will give notice of the application to the creditor and will allow representations to be made whether by phone or fax. On the order, which is made on form N37, the court may permit a bank or building society to make one or more payments out of the attached account and may specify the person to whom the payments should be made (for example, a landlord or mortgage lender) (CPR, r 72.7).

6.8 Effect of order and enforcement

If a final order is made, the third party should then pay over the judgment debt in accordance with the terms of the order. The creditor may first satisfy the costs of the procedure out of the sums received (CPR, r 72.11). The third party may retain a sum to cover the administrative expenses of compliance with the order (CCA 1981, s 109). This sum may be deducted even though there may not be enough to cover both the expenses and the judgment debt. Where the debt attached is in a bank or savings account, conditions attached to the account relating to withdrawals, such as the need to give notice or produce a pass book, do not apply to the payment out of sums under the order of the court (CCA 1981, s108 and SCA 1981, s 40).

Once the debt is paid, the third party is discharged of his/her liability to the judgment debtor (CPR, r 72.9). Note however, that if a sum in a foreign jurisdiction has been attached, a garnishee order may be refused if the law within that other jurisdiction does *not* provide for the discharge of the third party's liability through compliance with the court order. The courts have also held that there is no power to make pro-rata payments towards a number of liabilities due from the judgment debtor; the creditor who has priority in terms of obtaining the interim order will receive the available funds. Subsequent creditors may apply for their own orders but they will rank behind the creditor who is 'first past the post' (see *Société Eram Shipping Co Ltd v Compagnie Internationale de Navigation* [2004] AC 206, HL; *FG Hemisphere Associates LLC v Congo* [2005] EWHC 3201 (QB)).

If the third party does not pay, the order may be enforced against the debtor by execution like any other money judgment (CPR, r 72.9). If a building society or credit union account is attached, the court must allow a minimum balance of £1 to remain so that the defendant may remain a member of the institution (CPR, Part 72, PD, para 6).

A third party debt order may be subsequently set aside by the court and an order may be made requiring sums attached to be repaid. This may be done, for instance, where there has been an error made in the evidence supplied by the judgment creditor (see *Marshall v James* [1905] 1 Ch 432).

6.9 Monies in court

A third party debt order may not be made against money standing to the credit of the judgment debtor in court. Instead, the claimant may make application on notice for this sum, or sufficient of it to clear the judgment debt and costs, to be paid over to him. Notice of such an application must be served on the judgment debtor and the Accountant General at the Court Funds Office. Once an application for a payment from court funds is made, no money may be paid out of the court until the application has been heard.

7 Charging Orders and Related Remedies

7.1 Introduction

This remedy allows judgments in arrears to be secured against property. Charging orders will give the creditor confidence that the full judgment debt will probably eventually be cleared, but they do not guarantee ongoing instalment payment in the short term. It may be a considerable time before the secured asset is sold and, where the property involved forms the home for a spouse/partner and family, the court will seldom permit its sale. Of course, some debtors will not wish to have their ability to borrow against their property restricted in any way and may therefore act to discharge the judgment debt in full if a charging order is threatened.

The drawbacks to an application for a charging order include:

- the complexities and expense of the process. A Land Registry search will be necessary in advance to ascertain whether the property is solely or jointly owned and there are no pre-printed forms available from the court upon which to make the final application for an order for sale;

- the court will always give consideration to the proportionality of the application and may refuse to make a charge where there is a great disparity between the sum owed under the judgment and the value of the property; and

- the charge is only the halfway stage in the process. If the debtor does not continue to reduce the debt, a further application for an order for sale will be required, with the associated costs, and with the reduced likelihood that the court will be prepared to make the order requested.

Most of the discussion in this chapter concerns charging orders on land, which represent by far the largest proportion of orders made – indeed, the fact that a judgment debtor is a home owner and may be the subject of a charging order in due course is frequently the motivating factor for many creditors in initiating court action at all.

7.2 Chargeable assets

Under Charging Orders Act 1979 (COA 1979), s 2(1) one or more judgments may be secured by a charge against a capital asset owned by the judgment debtor whether solely, jointly or as a partnership. These assets include:

- any interest held beneficially by the debtor:
  - in land;
  - in securities such as government stock or stock in any company registered in England and Wales except a building society;
  - in funds in court;
  - in units in a unit trust;
  - in interest or dividends paid on securities, funds in court or unit trusts; or
  - under any trust.
- any interest held by a debtor as trustee of a trust:
  - where judgment was made against that person as a trustee of the trust; or
  - where the debtor holds the whole interest unencumbered for his/her own benefit; or
  - where joint trustees/debtors hold interest unencumbered for their own benefit.

Charging orders against securities cannot be made where the judgment debtor holds the stock as a trustee or personal representative. Conversely, if the securities are held by trustees on behalf of the judgment debtor, the debtor's interest may be charged. The issue of beneficial interest, especially in shares, may be complex and can require trial at court (see *Walker International Holdings Ltd v Congo* [2005] EWHC 2813 (Comm)).

As has been seen, a wide range of assets may be attached by charging order in theory. In reality, the huge majority of orders made are against land, for the simple reason of evidence. A large proportion of debtors will be home-owners and a search at the Land Registry can easily confirm this. The process is quick, the search form OS3 is simple to complete and Land Registry fee of £8 is nominal.

7.3 Application and interim order

A charging order may be sought at any time after the judgment was entered – no limitation period is imposed, although the court might refuse an order if it felt that there had been lengthy delay (see *Lowsley v Forbes* [1999] 1 AC 329).

If the judgment debtor has defaulted upon the terms of the judgment, an application for a charging order may be made to the court where the judgment was entered (unless the case has since been transferred to another county court, see CPR, r 73.3(2)) or, in the case of a charge on funds in court, to the court holding those funds (COA 1979, s 1).

Application will be made on form N379 in respect of land and form N380 in respect of securities. The applications will contain the following information:

- the name and address of the judgment debtor;
- the details of the judgment debt and the sums still due upon it;
- the amount of any instalments which have fallen due under the court's order for payment of the judgment debt;
- the existence of any other creditors of whom the applicant is aware; and
- the nature and ownership of the property (or properties) which are to be charged.

A copy of the relevant entry on the Land Register should be supplied with the form. This can be obtained by application on form OC1 with a payment of £8. In addition the applicant should provide two copies of a certificate giving details of interest accrued on judgments over £5000 and, if the judgment was made in the High Court, a copy of that order. A fee of £100 is payable. Charges over more than one asset may be sought in a single application; likewise, several judgments may be secured by a single charging order.

Providing that the DJ is satisfied with the application, an interim order will be made. Notice is then served on the interested parties, along with copies of the application and supporting evidence, giving at least twenty one days' notice of the hearing at which the making of the 'final' order will be considered. The parties who must receive notice of an interim charging order include:

- the judgment debtor,
- any co-owner of the property to be charged;
- any other named creditors;

112 Charging Orders and Related Remedies

- trustees of a trust;
- the keeper of the register of unit trusts;
- for funds in court, the Accountant General. Once service has been effected, no subsequent disposition of the funds will be valid against the judgment creditor; and
- in the case of securities, the Bank of England or the company concerned. After the date of service, no disposition of the securities by the debtor nor any payment of dividends or interest would be valid against the judgment creditor unless permission of the court had been obtained. If this provision of CPR, r 73.6 is breached, the judgment creditor will be entitled to receive the value of the securities transferred or the sums paid out, or the lesser sum necessary to discharge the judgment debt, from the person liable for the breach.

If the judgment creditor opts to serve the interim order, at the hearing for the final order service of the notice must be proved. This is done by the claimant by producing a copy of a certificate of service (form N215) which must have been filed in court not less than 2 days before the hearing. Proof of service is important: in one case a final order was refused because the defendant died after the making of the interim order but before its service upon him (see *Scott v Scott* [1952] 2 All ER 890). If the judgment debtor wishes to oppose the application, s/he may apply for it to be transferred to his/her local court.

7.4 Hearing

At the hearing the creditor must not only satisfy the court that a charge may be made, with details from the Land Registry, but must also satisfy the DJ that it is appropriate to make a charge in the circumstances of the debt and the debtor. The court has full discretion whether or not to make a final order, to discharge an interim charging order and to dismiss an application and to hear and determine any matters at issue between the parties or to direct their trial and to give directions for its conduct.

The judgment debtor may of course attend the hearing to oppose the interim order being confirmed, but correctly s/he must file and serve upon the creditor written grounds for the objection at least 7 days before the hearing date. In reality, DJs do not seem to insist upon this provision of CPR, r 73.8 and will hear the defendant in any case.

The court must consider all the circumstances of the case and, in particular, the personal circumstances of the debtor and whether any other creditors would be unduly prejudiced by the making of an order

Charging Orders and Related Remedies 113

(COA 1979, s 1(5)). In reality, most DJs do not give great weight to these considerations at this stage in the process. The general feeling appears to be that, if a creditor has a judgment outstanding against a defendant who owns property, then a charge should be made.

Charges should only be refused where:

- the debtor is insolvent. However, if there are joint debtors, only one of whom is insolvent, a charging order may be made against the other debtor's share of the property (see *Re Goldspan Ltd* [2003] BPIR 93, ChD; *Roberts Petroleum v Bernard Kenny Ltd* [1983] 1 All ER 564);
- another creditor has already initiated insolvency proceedings and/or insolvency appears to be imminent (see *Lewis v Eliades (No 5)*, ChD, 25 April 2005, unreported);
- the debt is very small compared to other sums owed by the debtor or compared to the value of the property or of the securities to be charged (see *Re Goldspan Ltd* [2003] BPIR 93, ChD; *Robinson v Bailey* [1942] Ch 268; *Wicks v Shanks* (1892) 67 LT 609);
- there may be serious prejudice to other creditors (see *Lewis v Eliades (No 5)*, ChD, 25 April 2005, unreported; *Nathan v Orchard* [2004] EWHC 344 (QB)); or
- the judgment is not actually in arrears (see *Mercantile Credit v Ellis* [1987] CLY 2917).

It is the last issue which has been the subject of prolonged controversy. A charging order is a form of execution – that is, it is a means of enforcing a judgment which is in arrears. It may be that only one instalment under a payment order has been missed – this is sufficient – but an application will not be possible if the original terms of the court order have been complied with or if the order has been varied and subsequently adhered to by the debtor (see *Ropaigealach v Allied Irish Bank* [2001] EWCA 1790 (Civ)).

Knowing that their judgment debtors may be occupying expensive properties, creditors have for a long time felt unhappy with this situation and have objected to the fact that they have been barred from seeking a charge to secure their interests by the mere fact that the debtor has been maintaining possibly small instalment payments on the judgment. DJs have long sympathised with this and the government took this on board in the Tribunals, Courts and Enforcement Act 2007 which contained provisions making it possible for creditors to seek charging orders without the need for there to have been default on a judgment. However, it has been decided not to introduce these provisions. Charging orders therefore remain a means of enforcing a judgment in

114 *Charging Orders and Related Remedies*

arrears. Creditors must therefore still resort to strategies which they have employed for some time to 'create' a default on a judgment. Where the court has ordered instalment payment, some creditors will make application to the court for a forthwith payment order to be substituted for the instalment order (see para 3.4). When the debtor fails to comply with this, they will be in default of payments and an application for a charge will be possible. Once again, many DJs are sympathetic to such applications. It must be left to the conscience of readers whether or not such a strategy should be attempted. It is arguable that such a course of action is not fully in accord with the overriding principles of the CPR, as extra work and expense are being created, but most county courts will go along with (if not actively facilitate) such proceedings.

Depending on the evidence as to circumstances it hears, the court may refuse an order, make the order 'final' or make a final order with conditions or modifications attached (COA 1979, s 3(1)). The most common alteration made by DJs is to make a charge but to stay its enforcement so long as instalment payments are maintained, but it might also be possible for the judgment debtor to persuade the court to impose other conditions. For example, enforcement of the charging order be postponed until a specific date, such as the date when the youngest child in the household ceases to be in full time education or to give time to complete the sale of the house, or enforcement could be stayed pending the determination of a cross claim made by the judgment debtor against the creditor (see *Austin-Fell v Austin-Fell, Midland Bank* [1990] 2 All ER 455; *Lewis v Eliades (No 5)*, ChD, 25 April 2005, unreported; *Shashoua v Sharma* [2009] EWHC 957 (Comm) – a 6-month stay on a charge to permit sale).

7.5 Effect of order

If the order is made final it takes effect from the date that the interim order was made. Notice is issued to the parties and all other creditors and co-owners who originally received notice of the interim order on form N87. The charge operates as if it were an equitable charge on the land made by the judgment debtor and provides the creditor with security for the order or judgment plus the costs of the application.

A charging order made against securities other than those held in court will include a stop notice unless the court orders otherwise (see para 7.7). If the securities subject to the charging order are held with more than one company, separate orders will be drawn up for each by the court.

It must be remembered that the charging order only affects the debtor's interest in the asset at the date that the interim order was made. Prior encumbrancers upon the property will not be prejudiced and may, of course, take their own enforcement action, regardless of the wishes of the judgment creditor. This will include mortgages upon a home as well as charging orders of an earlier date.

7.5.1 Land Registry

Where the judgment debtor is sole owner of the charged property, the order may be protected by the entry of a notice at the Land Registry (COA 1979, s 3(2)). This may be either an 'agreed notice' if the registered proprietor consents to the making of the charge or if the Registrar is satisfied that the claim is valid, or a 'unilateral notice' in all other cases. Application for the former will be on Land Registry form AN1 accompanied by a copy of the claim form and notice of issue, along with a fee of £50. Application for a unilateral notice is on form UN1. The claimant need only supply the fee plus a statement of the details of the charging order, the claim, case number and parties.

If the property is in joint ownership and the charge has been made against the share of only one of the co-owners, a restriction may be made on Form K. Application is on form RX1 (the application to enter a restriction) with the appropriate fee. If a judgment and charging orders have been entered against joint debtors, two separate applications will be required. The effect of form K is that no disposition of the registered estate will be capable of being registered without a certificate signed by the judgment creditor being produced which confirms that notice was given of the intended transaction. The registered owners of the property will receive notice of the application for the restriction on form B231; this gives them one month to object to the registration, otherwise it will be completed by the Land Registry.

Very occasionally, errors occur at the Land Registry, which may prejudice the rights of the judgment creditor. If these cannot be remedied by rectifying the register, it is possible to seek compensation or an indemnity for the Chief Land Registrar (see *Clark v Chief Land Registrar* [1993] Ch 294).

If a final charging order is refused at the hearing or is subsequently discharged by the court, the Land Registry entry will have to be cancelled as well by the judgment creditor.

7.5.2 Other enforcement

It is important to note that, as the charging order only provides security for the debt, rather than a means of directly producing repayment, the judgment creditor is not inhibited from pursuing other means of enforcement. If the court does not make a payment order or if the judgment debtor defaults upon the terms of payment, it will be permissible to consider recovery by any of the other means discussed in Chapters 4 to 6.

7.5.3 Variation or discharge of order

Under COA 1979, s 3(5) the debtor or any party interested in the property charged may apply to vary or discharge the order. The application must be made to the court in which the charging order was made. Notice will be served by the court upon all interested parties (CPR, r 73.4).

The debtor could make the application – for instance, where a judgment was subsequently set aside or where the judgment debt has been settled in full, including costs and interest (see set aside: *Brain v Herrick* [1894] 10 R 171; *Re Onslow's Trusts* [1875] 20 Eq 677; settled: *Mehta v Nolan*, QBD, 11 June 2009, unreported; *Al-Khayat v Al-Khayat* (2008) CLY 286 (ChD)). The court may exercise its discretion and set aside the charging order after taking into account all aspects of the parties' behaviour. Where the creditor, although secured, also proved in the debtor's bankruptcy and received dividends, whilst at the same time not seeking to enforce its security, the court felt justified in setting aside a charge. The court may also set aside orders because of procedural irregularities in the service of the original claim. Conversely, where an application to set aside judgment was made after a delay of 7 years and as a clear attempt to frustrate an application to enforce the debt by means of a charging order, the court refused to intervene (see *C & W Berry v Armstrong-Moakes* [2007] EWHC 2101 (QB); *Southern Aluminium & UPVC Windows Ltd v Clare*, CA, 20 May 1999, unreported; *Nolan v Devonport* [2006] EWHC 2025 (QB)).

A creditor may apply to vary a charging order where errors were made in the form of the original order – for example, by making an order charging the proceeds of sale under COA 1979, s 2(1)(a)(i) when in fact the land was held subject to a trust by joint owners, so that an order over the legal estate held under the statutory trust should have been made under s 2(1)(b). The court has discretion to rectify such minor procedural irregularities. An application to set aside may not be made by unsecured creditors of the judgment debtor, as they are unable to demonstrate any direct interest in the charge or any legal or equitable interest in the property (see *Clark v Chief Land Registrar* [1993] Ch 294; *Banque National de Paris v Montman Ltd* [2000] 1 BCLC 576).

Applications to set aside are often made by trustees in bankruptcy in order to maximise the estate available for the unsecured creditors in the insolvency. In principle a charge completed before the bankruptcy began – that is, before the bankruptcy order was made – should normally stand and should not be reversed (see *Nationwide Building Society v Wright* [2009] EWCA Civ 811). When deciding whether or not to grant such an application the court will consider such factors as:

- the time that has passed since the charging order was made and the consequent prejudice to the judgment creditor in question. Accordingly a charging order might be set aside when the bankruptcy followed by a matter of days, but if a year has elapsed, it would be unjust to set aside (see *National Westminster Bank v Caldeira* (1999) CLY 3225; *Jelle Zwemstra Ltd v Walton & Stewart* (1997) CLY 3002);
- the prejudice to other creditors arising from the charge, considering their own efforts to pursue the debt;
- whether the judgment creditor was aware of the pending insolvency; and
- compliance with the Insolvency Act 1986: a charge can be set aside where the judgment creditor has failed to seek permission of court before making the order final (see *Clarke v Coutts & Co* [2002] EWCA Civ 943).

The right to make application under this section also extends to the co-owning spouse of the debtor. This will enable such individuals to seek to postpone the effect of the order in order to protect their rights of occupation in a property (see *Harman v Glencross* [1986] Fam 81).

Finally, note that the correct manner of challenge to the making of a charging order is an appeal, *not* by way of judicial review.

7.6 Orders for sale

If the order is made absolute, it is still only a form of guarantee that the debt will be cleared at some unknown date in the future. A charging order is security for a judgment debt, but it is not an order enforcing it. If the creditor requires sooner payment, or if the debtor fails to make payments in line with the conditions attached by the court at the hearing, further proceedings will be needed to actually enforce the order (see *Jones v May* (2001) CLY 444, Cardiff County Court).

7.6.1 Limitations and orders for sale

Once made, it has been said that a charging order has a life of its own independent of the judgment (see *Ezekiel v Orakpo* [1997] 1 WLR 340,

CA). The Limitation Act 1980 does not apply and there is no limit upon when a charging order may be enforced. That said, though, there are limitations applicable to the amount of interest which may be recovered. Claims for arrears of interest are limited to sums due in period of 6 years up until the making of the original charging order. The charge will, however, also secure continuing interest until the principal debt is paid (see *Yorkshire Bank Finance v Mulhall* [2008] EWCA Civ 1156).

7.6.2 Application for an order for sale

If the charging is to be enforced, another application to the court will be necessary to obtain an order for sale. This will be an application by means of a Part 8 claim to the court which made the charging order (see Appendix 1.2, A, B and C for precedents for claims for orders for sale against securities and against solely and jointly owned properties). The claim may be supported by a witness statement (see Appendix 1.2, D for an example).

The application should include such details as:

- the date of final charging order;
- the amount for which the charge was made and the sums now due;
- the details of the asset(s) to be sold;
- the debtor's title to the property charged;
- any prior charges on the property;
- whether any other creditors are known; and
- an estimate of the market value of the property.

A copy of the original charging order must be filed with the claim form. Correctly, application for an order for sale in cases where the judgment exceeds £30,000 should be made in the Chancery Division of the High Court, but all such applications can be transferred to a county court for hearing by the High Court if this is more convenient for the parties (see *Wallace v Crossley* [2009] EWCA Civ 896; *National Westminster Bank v King* [2008] EWHC 280 (Ch)).

A fee of £150 is payable for this application. The court will set a hearing date and at least 21 days' notice is given to the respondents by serving the claim form upon them. The applicant receives notice of the hearing on form N206.

Charging Orders and Related Remedies 119

7.6.3 Application for a possession warrant

It is advisable for the application for an order for sale to be accompanied by a request for a possession warrant – although this application may be made subsequently if the defendant does not quit the property at the end of the period of 28 days given for compliance with the order. A warrant is required so that vacant possession can be ensured before sale of the property is completed. The request is made on court form N325. This is a short and simple application, merely requiring the creditor to provide the details of the order, the date upon which possession should have been surrendered (the date upon which the order for sale came into effect) and a description of the premises in question. A fee of £95 will also be payable.

7.6.4 Hearing of application

At this stage, the court has discretion whether or not to make an order. The court will give the greatest weight to the interests of the creditor but it will, nevertheless, give close consideration to the personal and financial situation of the debtor at this stage, even though arguments about those same issues may have been advanced but received short shrift at the hearing of the charging order. The debtor and other interested parties are very likely to be heard, even if they made no formal response to the order for sale application (see *Lloyds Bank v Byrne* [1993] 1 FLR 369, (1991) 23 HLR 472; *Harlow & Milner Ltd v Teasdale* [2006] EWHC 1708 (TCC)). Judges will be concerned with such matters as:

- the personal circumstances of the debtor;
- the reasons for the failure to pay;
- the prospects for repayment of the debt by instalments or other means;
- the interests of third parties (including other creditors);
- the ratio of debt to property value; and
- the level of any equity (COA 1979, s 3(4)).

Even so, the court will remain conscious of the right of the creditor to be paid and the fact that postponing sale will mean continued exposure to 'the vagaries of the property market and the possibility of adverse swings in value' (see *Society of Lloyds v Surman* [2004] EWHC 2967 (Ch)) Accordingly, payment from the defendant(s) will generally be expected during the term of any suspension and the stay may be for a limited period, subject to review or to the outcome of other events (see *National Westminster Bank v Rushmer* [2010] EWHC 554 (Ch) – a stay for

21 months, or until litigation likely to produce a substantial lump sum was completed, subject to payment of £2666).

In recent years, the argument has several times been advanced that the making of an order for sale would constitute a breach of the rights of the debtor or other occupier under the European Convention on Human Rights (ECHR). The courts have rejected these arguments. In enforcing a charging order, there is no breach of either ECHR, Art 8 or First Protocol, Art 1 (the right to protection of family life and the right to enjoyment of property). This is because the procedure for making an order for sale is in accordance with the law and such enforcement is in the public interest because of the economic importance of enforcing debt obligations (see *C Putnam & Sons v Taylor* [2009] EWHC 317 (Ch); *Close Invoice Finance Ltd v Pile* [2008] EWHC 1580 (Ch)). This should especially be the case where a jointly owned property is involved, as then the court will also exercise its discretion under Trusts for Land and Appointment of Trustees Act 1996, ss 14 and 15, which should normally be sufficient to satisfy the demands of the ECHR (see para 7.6.5) (see *National Westminster Bank v Rushmer* [2010] EWHC 554 (Ch)).

Even at this late stage in recovery proceedings, the court has the discretion to put off actual sale of the property even when awarding the judgment creditor an order for sale. The court may postpone sale of the house until a specified later date – for example, after a dependent child's 18th birthday or in order to allow the family time to sell the property themselves and find alternative accommodation (see *Close Invoice Finance Ltd v Pile* [2008] EWHC 1580 (Ch); *C Putnam & Sons v Taylor* [2009] EWHC 317 (Ch)). Equally, the court can suspend the order for sale and may well do so on terms of the debtor making instalment payment, both to afford the person a last chance to pay and also to protect the interests of the execution creditor (see *National Westminster Bank v Rushmer* [2010] EWHC 554 (Ch)).

7.6.5 Jointly owned properties

Where the property is jointly owned, the charging order takes effect against the judgment debtor's beneficial interest in the property (see *National Westminster Bank v Stockman* [1981] 1 All ER 800). The creditor then becomes a party with an interest in the property and, as such, has the right, under Trusts for Land and Appointment of Trustees Act 1996, s 14 to apply for an order for sale so as to realise that share in the premises. If such an application is made, s 15 of the 1996 Act requires the court to take into account extra considerations over and above those which might arise under the terms of the COA 1979 (these provisions of the 1996 Act do not apply to solely owned properties: *Wells v Pickering*

[2000] EWHC 2540 (Ch)). These include:

- the intentions of the co-owners at the time of purchase of the property. If the property was purchased as a family home, the court may choose to respect this intention until such time as this need has passed (see *Lloyds Bank v Shorney* [2001] EWCA Civ 1161);
- the welfare of any dependent child occupying the property as his/her home; and
- the interests of any secured creditor. An order for sale may be made where equity is available to discharge some of the secured amount, albeit not the whole sum due, if the debtor is unable otherwise to clear the debt (see *Bank of Ireland v Bell* [2001] FLR 809, CA; *The Mortgage Corporation Ltd v Shaire* [2001] Ch 743).

Joint owners will be notified of the applications for a charge and an order for sale and they will be entitled to attend the hearing in order to make representations to the court. The court's orders should only be set aside in exceptional circumstances – where for example the spouse had no proper opportunity to make representations.

If the owners of the property in question are married, but are in the process of divorcing, the outcome of the order for sale application will be determined in part by the stage that the divorce proceedings have reached. If proceedings have begun in the family court the decision on the order for sale may be adjourned to be heard at the same time as other questions relating to the couple's property and finances. Alternatively, a charging order may be made, with a stay imposed upon its enforcement until the matrimonial issues have been resolved (see *First National Securities Ltd v Hegerty* [1985] QB 850).

7.6.6 Sale of properties

If an order is made, it is issued by the court on form N436. The defendant is given 28 days to clear the debt or to vacate the property. The execution creditor has a degree of latitude as to the timing and method of the sale. Once a mode of sale is chosen, the property should be properly marketed in an appropriate manner. As long as the sale is genuine, the creditor is entitled to have regard to his/her own interests as creditor in its conduct (see *Bell v Long* [2008] EWHC 1273 (Ch)).

Once sale is completed, and after all prior charges on the property plus the outstanding judgment debt and costs have been cleared, the balance will be paid into court. The creditor may discharge all sums due under the judgment as well as all statutory interest accrued up to 6 years before the date of the making of the charging order and all interest which has accrued upon the charge since that date (see *Yorkshire Bank Finance v Mulhall* [2008] EWCA Civ 1156).

7.7 Stop orders and notices

The purpose of stop orders and notices is no longer as clear, under the modern rules of court, as was originally the case. Both now are applicable to both funds in court and to securities. In the past stop orders were made in respect of funds in court and stop notices were issued in respect of stocks and shares. This distinction is still a helpful guide to their use.

A charging order on registered land is protected by a notice at the Land Registry, which ensures that the charge is cleared from the proceeds of sale when the property is sold. Stop orders and notices have similar functions in respect of securities and funds in court. For instance, stop orders may protect the rights of mortgagees of funds in court and stop notices function by alerting the court to the applicant's rights. This procedure can be especially useful where the securities stand in the name of a third party, such as a trustee of the judgment debtor (see *Stuart v Cockerell* (1869) 8 Eq 607; *Lister v Tidd* (1867) 4 Eq 462).

Under COA 1979, s 5(5), both stop orders and notices inhibit the following transactions:

- the transfer, sale, delivery out, payment or any other dealings with funds in court;
- the registration of a transfer of the securities;
- the payment out of dividends or interest on securities; or
- the acquisition of or dealings with units in a unit trust.

7.7.1 Stop notices

A stop notice may be included in a final charging order under CPR, r 73.8(3) or may be sought by application in the High Court. If a notice is made it should give complete protection to a person claiming a beneficial interest in securities by ensuring that notice of any intended transfer or payment is served upon him/her. The notice ensures that the creditor receives warning of dealings, but it will probably still be necessary for further action to be taken, whether that is an application for an injunction or a stop order.

An application to the Court should include a draft copy of the notice the judgment creditor wishes the court to issue (see Appendix 1.3, A) along with evidence identifying the securities in question, the applicant's interest in them and an address for service of the notice. If the application has been correctly made, a court officer will issue the notice – which the applicant must then serve.

The notice takes effect when it is served and remains in force until it is withdrawn or discharged. It prohibits the dealings described above unless the person on whom it was served gives 14 days' notice to the applicant. After the expiry of this period of notice, if the creditor has not taken further steps the bank or company subject to the stop notice may carry through the instructions received and may deal with the funds or securities in question (see *Ex parte Amyot* (1841) 1 Ph 130n; *Adam v Bank of England* (1908) 52 Sol Jo 682).

Notices may be withdrawn by serving a written request on the court and the person served with the stop notice. The court may also order discharge of a notice on application from any person interested in the securities.

7.7.2 Stop orders

A stop order will generally be made automatically by the court as part of any final charging order which is issued in respect of securities other than those held in court (CPR, r 73.8(3)). Separate application may be made by a judgment creditor to the High Court under CPR, r 73.12. The orders may be made in respect of the following assets:

- *funds in court*, on application from any person with a charge upon them or who is a judgment creditor of the person entitled to them. Note that, whilst a prior court order is not essential, a stop order in the absence of a pre-existing charging order may not give the creditor sufficient protection (see *Shaw v Hudson* (1879) 48 LJ Ch 689; *Hopewell v Barnes* [1876] 1 Ch D 630); or

- *securities*, on application from a person claiming a beneficial interest in them.

A stop order should give compete protection to a judgment creditor by preventing dealings with funds and securities without notice being served upon him/her. In respect of funds in court, it is not usually necessary to follow up a charging order with a stop order, as notice of the charge to the Accountant General will generally be sufficient. However, if the funds stand to the account of a third party it may be wise to take the extra precaution. Stop orders can only be made in respect of ascertained sums, so if the funds are subject to detailed assessment, the application will not succeed (see *Brereton v Edwards* [1888] 21 QBD 488, CA; *Widgery v Tepper* (1877) 6 ChD 364).

Application is made on notice in existing proceedings or by a Part 8 claim if there are no existing court proceedings. See Appendix 1.3, B and C for specimen applications for stop orders upon securities and upon funds in courts and also for a sample witness statement in support of the application. The claim form must be served on every person affected by the order and on the Accountant General at the Court Funds Office in the case of applications respecting court funds.

A stop order prohibits the any of the dealings described earlier with the funds in court, and any income upon them, or with the securities. An order made in respect of securities must identify those securities, the name in which they stand, the dealings which are prohibited and whether dividends and interest are affected. In relation to each other and in insolvency, orders have priority according to the date on which they are made (see *In re Holmes* (1885) 29 Ch D 786; *Palmer v Locke* (1880) 18 Ch D 381).

An order may be discharged or varied on application to the court by any person interested in the securities. The application should be made on notice on form N244 and copies should be served upon all interested parties (see Appendix 1.3, E for a sample application) (see CPR, r 73.15).

7.8 Partnership property

Under Partnership Act 1890, s 23 execution may not be issued against partnership property unless the judgment is against the firm. Instead, the High Court or a county court on application from the judgment creditor may make a charging order against the partner's interest in the partnership property and profits. This charge will be for the judgment debt and any accruing interest, and it may also include orders appointing a receiver of the profits and directing that accounts are produced. It is important in such proceedings to ensure that all applications and orders are served upon all partners within England and Wales, although the Practice Direction to CPR, Part 73 provides that, if a document is served upon one or more partners, it will be regarded as having been served upon all.

7.9 Receivers by way of equitable execution

A final and little used means of enforcement that may occasionally be of utility is the receiver by way of equitable execution. This power is available in county courts under CCA 1981, s 107 and Senior Courts Act 1981, s 37. It enables a judgment creditor to enforce a judgment by appointing a receiver in respect of all the debtor's legal estates and interests in land or other property, whether legal or beneficial.

The expanded scope of charging orders has reduced the scope of receiverships, but the procedure could still be employed where the judgment debtor has a beneficial interest in a sum of money which is not necessarily a debt but which is held by, or is about to be paid out by, some person to or upon the behalf of the judgment debtor. This is likely to be future receipts from a particular asset, which may include:

- income such as rents and other profits from property s/he owns;
- future debts which would not be attachable by a third party debt order;
- an equitable interest in a property as a tenant for life;
- leasehold property subject to a mortgage; or
- where leasehold or freehold property is subject to a contract for sale (see *Masri v Consolidated Contractors International UK Ltd & others (No 2)* [2008] EWCA Civ 303).

A receiver could be appointed in order to receive a single sum of money, several lump sum payments or ongoing payments over a period of time. A receiver may be appointed in respect of land even though a charging order has also be made, securing the judgment on the same property. Amongst the sources of income which may not be attached are a judgment debtor's entitlements under a private pension scheme (see *Field v Field* [2003] 1 FLR 376).

7.9.1 Application to court

Application may be made under CPR, Part 69 without notice on form N244. The application must be supported by written evidence. This supporting evidence should:

- explain why a receiver is required;
- give details of the judgment being enforced and the extent to which the debtor has defaulted upon its terms;
- give details of other steps taken already to enforce the judgment and why any attempting other means of enforcement is considered to be inappropriate;
- provide details of the property to be affected. This should include estimates of the property's value and of the amount of income likely to be produced; and

- supply full details of the person to be appointed as receiver, demonstrating his/her fitness to undertake the role. Written evidence from a person acquainted with the nominated receiver must disclose whether s/he is believed to be suitable to take on the role – and why. A receiver must be an individual; licenced insolvency practitioners often undertake this work as they will already have in place suitable bonds to cover them for such responsibilities. The nominee's signed consent to take on the role should also be included with the application (see *Capewell v Customs & Excise* [2004] EWCA Civ 1628 for some helpful guidelines on the form of the application to the court).

An injunction may be sought at the same time and on the same application in order to prevent dealings with the property in question until the receiver has been appointed.

7.9.2 Appointment by court

The decision whether or not to appoint a receiver is entirely at the court's discretion. The court has complete control of the post and may dismiss and replace the receiver if it thinks fit. The person appointed may be a trustee, a solicitor or even the judgment creditor (though this is usually only permitted where relatively small amounts are due under the judgment and on the basis that no remuneration will be claimed). If a person other than a court officer is appointed to act as receiver, s/he will only be allowed to take up the post once security, or an indemnity from the judgment creditor, has been provided to ensure that s/he will account for what is received. The amount of the receiver's remuneration and the mode of payment, the duty to submit accounts, dealings with payments received and the right to seek the directions of the court will be set out by the court order (see *Re Ward* (1862) 31 Beav 1).

The court will take into account a number of factors when deciding whether to appoint a receiver. It must be satisfied that the appointment is just and convenient and it must have regard to relative proportion between the judgment debt and the receiver's probable expenses and receipts. Accordingly, the court may refuse to order the appointment where the debt is too small or nominal and where it is considered likely that the costs incurred will be disproportionate to the sums to be recovered. Where the debt is relatively small, conditions may be attached regarding the costs of the receivership (see *I v K* (1884) WN 63). This is especially likely to be the case if another means of enforcement could be employed instead.

The resulting court order will generally include provisions as to the form and amount of security to be provided by the receiver appointed;

detailed provision as to the remuneration of the receiver (who will pay, how payment will be made and the rate of remuneration, taking into account the complexity and scale of the case) and the details of accounts which the receiver may be required to produce whether periodically or at the conclusion of the receivership.

7.9.3 Effect of order

The order appointing a receiver is served upon the nominee, the other parties to the case and any other person the court directs. The receiver appointed by the court will then deal with the specified property, collecting the income or proceeds and paying over those sums into court as ordered. The property does not vest in the receiver; instead the order operates as an injunction preventing others taking possession of the assets.

A receiver may seek directions on the conduct of the receivership from the court whilst the court may dismiss a receiver for failing to comply with the rules of the CPR, the practice directions or the terms of the court's orders.

Appendix 1
Prescribed Forms and Precedents

1.1 Letter before action

The practice direction requires that a letter before action provides:

- the full name and address of the claimant;
- a reasonably full statement of the basis for the claim;
- a clear summary of the facts upon which the claim is based;
- what the claimant wants from the defendant. If money is demanded, an explanation of how it has been calculated should be provided. This may be a simple sum of money and interest, but for damages claims it should set out the different losses which will be claimed with an indication of the how compensation under each may be calculated;
- a list of the key documents upon which the claimant will rely;
- a suggestion of the most suitable forms of **ADR** and an invitation to try to settle the dispute by this means. This may just be an indication that the claimant is prepared to enter discussions with the defendant;
- a date by which a reply is expected – that is, 2 weeks to respond in full to a straightforward claim or 2 weeks to send an acknowledgment in cases of greater complexity;
- a request for copies of any documents in the possession of the defendant which the claimant wishes to see.
- it is good practice to provide details as to how payment of any debt should be made and to provide contact details so that payment can be discussed and arranged;
- it is also good practice to refer an individual defendant for advice, so example to a Citizens Advice Bureau, and to allow a reasonable time of (say) 14 days for the person to obtain advice before responding.

1.2 Applications for orders for sale

A Part 8 claim – sole owner

Details of claim

The claimant claims:

1   On (date) in claim number [ ] the court (or [ ] county court) granted the claimant a final charging order securing £[ ], the sum at that date due under the judgment debt and costs, upon the defendant's freehold (or leasehold) interest in the property known as (address).

2   The defendant has made no payments (or payments of only £) in respect of the outstanding judgment debt and costs and the balance remaining due from the defendant as of (date) is £[ ], upon which interest accrues at the rate of £[ ] daily.

3   The claimant therefore claims an order that:

   a   The defendant's property at (address) which is subject to the final charging order in favour of the claimant shall be sold without further reference to the court and for a price not less than £[ ] (unless that figure is altered by further order of the court);

   b   The claimant's solicitor shall have conduct of the sale;

   c   To enable the claimant to conduct the sale, there shall be created and vested in the claimant, pursuant to Law of Property Act 1925, s 90, a legal term in the property of 3000 years (or of one day less than the period remaining upon the term of the lease under which the defendant holds the property, which is for a term of [ ] years created by (under)lease between [ ] and [ ] and dated [ ]);

   d   The defendant shall deliver up possession of the property to the claimant; and

   e   The claimant shall apply the proceeds of sale as follows:

      i   To pay the costs and expenses of conducting the sale;

      ii   To discharge any charges or other securities upon the property which enjoy priority over the charging order;

      iii To retain the sum due to the claimant at the date of sale; and

      iv   To pay the balance (if any) to the defendant (or into court, or as the court shall direct).

4   The defendant shall pay the claimant's costs of this claim.

CPR, Part 8 applies to this claim.

B   Part 8 claim – joint owners/defendants

Details of claim

The claimant claims:

1 On (date) in claim number [ ] the court (or [ ] county court) granted the claimant a final charging order securing £[ ], the sum at that date due under the judgment debt and costs, upon the first defendant's beneficial interest in the freehold (or leasehold) property, known as (address), which is vested in the joint names of the defendants.

2 The first defendant has made no payments (or payments of only £[ ]) in respect of the outstanding judgment debt and costs and the balance remaining due from the first defendant as of (date) is £[ ], upon which interest accrues at the rate of £[ ] daily.

3 The claimant therefore claims an order that:

   a The defendants' property at (address) which is subject to the final charging order in favour of the claimant shall be sold without further reference to the court and for a price not less than £[ ] (unless that figure is altered by further order of the court);

   b The claimant's solicitor shall have conduct of the sale;

   c Under Trustee Act 1925, s 50 the court shall appoint the claimant (or the claimant's solicitor) to convey the property;

   d The defendants shall deliver up possession of the property to the claimant; and

   e The claimant shall apply the proceeds of sale as follows:

      i   To pay the costs and expenses of conducting the sale;

      ii   To discharge any charges or other securities upon the property which enjoy priority over the charging order;

      iii To divide the remaining proceeds into two equal shares, paying one equal share to the second defendant and, out of the other equal share, retaining the sum due from the first defendant to the claimant at the date of sale; and

      iv   To pay the balance (if any) to the first defendant (or into court, or as the court shall direct).

4 The first defendant shall pay the claimant's costs of this claim.

CPR, Part 8 applies to this claim.

C Part 8 claim – for order for sale of securities

Details of claim

The claimant claims:

1 On (date) in claim number [ ] the court (or [ ] county court) granted the claimant a judgment for the amount of £[ ], being the sum at that date due from the defendant.

2 On (date) the court made a final charging order under which the stock or shares of [ ] plc which stand in the name of the defendant are to stand charged with the payment to the claimant of the sum of £[ ] and £[ ] costs.

3 The defendant has made no payments (or payments of only £) in respect of the outstanding judgment debt and costs and the balance remaining due from the defendant as of (date) is £[ ], upon which interest accrues at the rate of £[ ] daily.

4 The claimant therefore claims an order that:

   a The stocks and share mentioned in paragraph (2), or sufficient of them as shall discharge the defendant's liability to the claimant (including the costs of this claim), shall be sold without further reference to the court and for a price not less than £[ ] (unless that figure is altered by further order of the court);

   b The claimant's solicitor shall have conduct of the sale;

   c The defendant shall deliver up possession of the stocks or shares to the claimant;

   d The defendant shall sign the deeds or documents necessary to effect the sale; and

   e The claimant shall apply the proceeds of sale as follows:

      i To pay the costs and expenses of conducting the sale;

      ii To discharge any charges or other securities upon the property which enjoy priority over the charging order;

      iii To retain the sum due to the claimant at the date of sale; and

      iv To pay the balance (if any) to the defendant (or into court, or as the court shall direct).

5 The defendant shall pay the claimant's costs of this claim.

CPR, Part 8 applies to this claim.

D Witness statement supporting a claim for an order for sale of a jointly owned property

Witness statement

I (name) of [ ], solicitors for the claimant, wish to rely upon the following evidence in support of the claimant's claim for an order for sale:

1. On (date) in claim number [ ] the court (or [ ] county court) granted the claimant a judgment for the amount of £[ ], being the sum at that date due from the defendant including costs.

2. On (date) in claim number [ ] the court (or [ ] county court) granted the claimant a final charging order securing £[ ], the sum at that date due under the judgment debt and costs, upon the first defendant's beneficial interest in the freehold (or leasehold) property, known as (address), which is vested in the joint names of the defendants. A copy of the order is exhibit 1.

3. The first defendant has made no payments (or payments of only £) in respect of the outstanding judgment debt and costs and the balance remaining due from the first defendant as of (date) is £[ ], upon which interest accrues at the rate of £[ ] daily.

4. The title to the property is registered at HM District Land Registry under title number [ ]. I refer to exhibit 2, a set of office copies of the entries on the Register showing that the first defendant is proprietor of the named property jointly with the second defendant (name) with a freehold (or leasehold) estate.

OR

The title to the property is unregistered and I refer to exhibit 2, an examined epitome (or abstract) of title which shows that the legal freehold (or leasehold) title to the property is vested in the first and second defendants jointly. [Amend as necessary for sole owners]

5. By virtue of the charging order, the claimant is a person interested in the proceeds of sale of the property and, accordingly, is entitled to apply to the court under Trusts of Land and Appointment of Trustees Act 1996, s 14. [Miss out for sole owners]

6. So far as the claimant is aware, the only other creditors with prior charges or security over the property in question are as follows:

    a The [ ] Building Society have a first legal charge in order to secure the sum of £[ ] and I am informed that the balance due is £[ ];

134 Appendix 1

    b [ ] Homeloans have a second legal charge on the property to secure the sum of £[ ] and I am informed that the balance due is £[ ]; and

    c [ ] Finance have registered a final charging order and I am informed that the balance due is £[ ];

7 Exhibit 3 is a valuation of the property which has been obtained from [ ] Estate Agents and which indicates that the property is likely to sell for £[ ].

8 So far as the claimant is aware, the only persons in possession of the property are the first and second defendants and their family. [OR the defendant and his/her spouse and children]

9 I am informed and believe that the property was purchased by the defendants as a home for themselves and their family. The ages of the children are[ ] and [ ].

OR

The property is a residential property and a Class F land charge (or a notice under Family Law Act 1996, s 31(10)) has been registered on behalf of (name) and I confirm that notice of this claim will be served upon him/her.

1.3 Stop orders and notices

A Draft stop notice

TO – [the person to whom the notice is addressed]

TAKE NOTICE THAT [name and address of applicant]

Claims to be beneficially interested to an interest in the following securities:

[specify here the securities in question and in whose name they stand]

This notice requires you to refrain from:

1   registering a transfer of the securities identified above; and

2   paying any dividend or interest in respect of those securities,

without giving 14 days notice to the said [insert name] of the above address.

B Application for a stop order on securities (N244)

The claimant intends to apply for:

1   A stop order in respect of the securities specified in the next paragraph;

2   The order is sought in respect of the following securities [specify];

3   These securities stand in the name of [ ];

4   The stop order is for a prohibition applicable to the securities (and/or the dividends or interest upon them);

5   The steps which it is sought to prohibit are:

   a   The registration of any transfer of the securities;

   b   The making of any payment by way of dividend, interest or otherwise in respect of those securities; and/or

   c   In respect of those securities which consist of units of a unit trust, any acquisition of, or other dealings with, the units by any person or body exercising functions under the trust.

The claimant wishes to rely upon the attached witness statement in support of this application.

C Application for a stop order on funds in court (N244)

The claimant intends to apply for:

An order, a draft of which is attached, that no part of the capital funds in court [identify] to the credit of the defendant, and that no part of any dividends or interest accruing on the said funds to which the defendant is (or may become) entitled, shall be transferred, sold, delivered out, paid or otherwise dealt with without further order of the court.

The claimant wishes to rely upon the attached witness statement in support of this application.

D Witness statement in support of request for a stop notice

Witness statement

I [name] of [ ], solicitors for the applicant, wish to rely upon the following evidence in support of the applicant's claim for stop notice under CPR, r 73.17:

1 The securities in respect of which the applicant seeks a stop notice are as follows [describe].

2 [Lay out how the applicant's interest arises in the securities].

3 The address for service of the applicant is [ ].

4 A draft stop notice in the form set out in Appendix B of the Practice Direction to CPR, Part 73 is attached to this application. (see para A, above).

E Application to vary a stop notice (N244)

The claimant intends to apply for an order in the following terms:

1 That the stop notice issued by the court on [date], at the request of the above named claimant, to stop the transfer of the securities mentioned therein, and served upon the Governor of the Bank of England, be varied as set out below;

2 That the following variation(s) shall be made to the stop notice [set out terms of the variation]; and,

3 That the defendant shall pay the claimant's costs of this application.

Appendix 2
Useful Addresses

Credit reference agencies

The main agencies are as follows:

- Equifax, Augustus House, 3, New Augustus Street, Bradford, BD1 5LL;
- Experian, Landmark House, Experian Way, NG2 Business Park, Nottingham, NG80 1ZZ; and
- CallCredit, One Park Lane, Leeds, LS3 1EP.

Registry Trust Ltd

Registry Trust administers the register of court judgment which may be search for information on debtors. It may be contacted at:

- Registry Trust Ltd, 153–157, Cleveland Street, London W1T 6QW.

See its website:

- www.trustonline.org.uk

Other jurisdictions

Northern Ireland Court Service:

- www.courtsni.gov.uk

Scotland:

- Court Service: www.scotcourts.gov.uk; and
- Registers of Scotland: www.ros.gov.uk

HCEOA

High Court Enforcement Officers Association Limited:

- HCEOA Limited, PO Box 180, Winsford, CW7 2WP.

Her Majesty's Courts Service

The HM Courts Service website is a valuable source of information, as it has available upon it the CPR, downloadable copies of all county court forms and other useful information on court addresses, court fees and the like:

- www.hm-courtservice.gov.uk

Also useful is the online issue service at:

- www.moneyclaim.gov.uk

Insolvency forms

Insolvency forms are available to download from the Insolvency Service website:

- www.insolvency.gov.uk/forms